"Shelter from the Storm"

FREDERICK

MARYLAND

*A Place of Refuge in the
Seven Year's War*

Robert Kozak

HERITAGE BOOKS
2008

HERITAGE BOOKS

AN IMPRINT OF HERITAGE BOOKS, INC.

Books, CDs, and more—Worldwide

For our listing of thousands of titles see our website
at
www.HeritageBooks.com

Published 2008 by
HERITAGE BOOKS, INC.
Publishing Division
100 Railroad Ave. #104
Westminster, Maryland 21157

International Standard Book Number: 978-0-7884-4568-2

This book is dedicated to the people who are providing aid and shelter to the refugees of wars in the 21st Century. From Kosovo to Darfur and too many places in between, their daily work of helping their fellow humans should be honored by all.

Table of Contents

List of Illustrations

Foreward

We are in the midst of the 250 Year Commemoration of the Seven Years War 1756-1763, considered by many historians to be the First World War of the modern era. Long and bloody battles were fought on the North American, European, and Asian continents. Major sea battles were fought in the Caribbean and off the coast of India. It resulted in the creation of the British Empire and set the stage for major political changes in Europe.

In the United States it is usually called the French and Indian War, if it is remembered at all. In North America the Seven Years War was a desperate "Clash of Empires" between Native American Tribes trying to regain their territories, the French and English trying to claim them, and American settlers who for the first time saw themselves as an independent nation. Changing goals and changing alliances were a constant in the North American part of the war.

The Seven Years War was also a training ground for the American Revolution. George Washington and Benjamin Franklin were major characters in both. Others such as Daniel Boone and Daniel Morgan gained their first combat experience in the Seven Years War. And the taxes placed on the colonists to fund the war, the Stamp Act, etc., were the specific causes for the start of the Revolution.

When I start talking about the Seven Years War, I'm surprised by the general lack of knowledge about it. But I guess this is in large part because of a lack of exposure. After all there hasn't been an "eight-part Ken Burns PBS documentary" about it.

Throughout New York and Pennsylvania many local historical groups are making major efforts through commemorative events to try to change this situation. I'd like to especially point out: The Conococheague Institute in Welsh Run, Pennsylvania, The National Park Service which has built a beautiful and very informative new visitor's center at Ft. Necessity National Battlefield near Farmington Pennsylvania, and The Braddock's Field Historical Society in Braddock, Pennsylvania that has purchased land where Braddock's forces were defeated at the Battle of the Monongahela and are pushing to build a museum to tell the story of that very important event. Appendix IV contains contact information for these and other organizations that are working hard to tell the story of the Seven Years War.

Another part of the problem of bringing the Seven Years War to life is the lack of structures and unchanged landscapes from that era. It is hard to visualize a battle when the battlefield is now in the middle of an urban neighborhood. Fortunately, Frederick, Maryland has a very unique building, Schifferstadt, whose initial construction is a result of the Seven Years War.

Using Schifferstadt as a starting point, I've tried to write the story of Frederick in the Seven Years War by synthesizing the information that has been collected by others with my own research focusing on the role of Frederick as a refugee center and the similarities in Seven Year War fortified house architecture throughout North America.

Think of this book as the first draft of that history. I hope it will encourage and challenge readers to find out more, and maybe to do some of their own research. I also hope it will encourage government officials to look more positively on the potential of Seven Years War tourism and to put more resources into the preservation and interpretation of sites from that time period.

I'd like to thank Joanne Ivancic for her help and support. Without it this book would never have gotten done. I'd also like to thank the Conococheague Institute for its help and especially their Executive Director Walter Powell for his help, suggestions, and thorough review.

My guides in historical research and writing about history are Simon Schama and Ivor Noel Hume. I recommend all of their books.

The opinions expressed in this book are solely mine, as are the mistakes.

Robert Kozak
Frederick, Maryland
2007

Some Notes on Names and Locations

Until the American Revolution, Frederick County comprised all of Maryland west and north of Georgetown DC. Frederick County contained all the land now in Montgomery, Carroll, Washington, Allegany, Garrett, and of course Frederick counties.

The term Fredericktown is used for Frederick in this book. This is the terminology used by Maryland Governor Horatio Sharpe during the time period to distinguish it from Frederick County. I think its use seems fitting.

The terms Great Valley, Cumberland Valley, and Shenandoah Valley all refer to the same valley that is west of South Mountain in Pennsylvania and Maryland and the Blue Ridge in Virginia. Present day US 11 and I-81 follow the general route of the north-south Native trails. During the Civil War this route was called the Valley Turnpike and was used by the Confederates to invade Pennsylvania in June of 1863 prior to the battle of Gettysburg.

The term Indian is used in the accounts written at the time and in most 18-20th Century histories of the "French and Indian War." For that reason, it will be used in this book. No offense is meant in the use of this term.

Wherever possible, the contemporary name for a location is included, usually in parentheses, since place names have changed over the past 250 years. Probably the place mentioned in this book with the most name changes is "Forks of the Ohio" (Ft. Duquesne 1754-658) (Ft. Pitt 1758-mid 1770s) (Pittsburgh mid-1770s to present).

All photos, unless noted, are by Joanne Ivancic.

Introduction: Going Back in Time

The large stone building pictured below is called Schifferstadt. It is located hard by an elevated freeway (US 15) in Frederick Maryland, a rapidly growing city of about 60,000 less than fifty miles west of Washington DC. Without any roadside sound barriers in place, it's hard to hear anyone speak outside, especially when the trees are without leaves. A family called the Brunners, who had emigrated from the Upper Rhine Valley in Germany in 1729, built it between 1756 and 1758. The fieldstone building is about 30 feet by 40 and has walls almost two feet think. Underneath the building is a large, vaulted cellar that is entered directly from the outside so that large barrels, farm equipment, and produce can be quickly stored.

It's hard to visualize what the countryside must have looked when it was built. Making it even harder, the creek that used to curve within about sixty feet of the south side of the building was straightened and relocated to the south when the US 15 bypass was built in the 1950s. The building itself also has changed. In the 1800s, a large brick two-story addition was built on the south side of the stone building that included an expanded kitchen and a dairy. Furthermore, a recent architectural survey revealed that the west side exterior door and several windows were added to the original stone structure sometime after it was built.

But, even with all these changes, let's try to imagine what the Brunner farm looked like when their new house called Schifferstadt was first built. Look at that picture again. Imagine fewer windows, and those that were there were smaller and were equipped with thick shutters. There wouldn't have been trees surrounding it, being freshly cleared farmland. Looking west, where US 15 now is, were two more farms owned by the Brunners, comprised of about 600 acres. The view to the west was dominated by Catoctin Mountain that runs from the southwest to the northeast. This is the first ridge of the Appalachian range. The summit is about six miles from Schifferstadt. The ridgeline varies in elevation from 800 feet to 1800 feet. The highest section is clearly visible from the farm, just slightly to the north. Catoctin Mountain joins with South Mountain about fifteen miles north forming a "V" shaped valley. This is the Middletown Valley. Just west of South Mountain is the Great Valley. It runs from central Pennsylvania to eastern Tennessee. In Pennsylvania and Maryland it is called the Cumberland Valley. In Virginia and West Virginia it is the Shenandoah Valley. The western side of the Cumberland Valley is bordered by Tuscarora Mountain that runs north from the Potomac River through Maryland and into Pennsylvania.

Tribal hunting parties still traversed the Great Valley in the early 1750s. Under treaty arrangements, they still had access to wild game, and traditional campgrounds around natural springs. To maintain these claims, Iroquois leaders encouraged year round settlement.

Fredericktown and the area east of Catoctin Mountain had once been the home to many Native Tribal settlements. However, there hadn't been any Native American occupation for at least fifty years due to overhunting and encroaching English settlements. The last Indian groups to spend anytime here were the Tuscarora in the 1720s. They were passing through on their journey from their homeland in the Carolinas and Virginia to western New York, where they would become the sixth and final tribe to join the Iroquois Confederation. Two creeks near Fredericktown, one north and one south of town, are called Tuscarora, named to recognize where they camped. That basically unhappy journey was caused by the expansion of English settlements in Virginia and the broken treaties and warfare that accompanied the expansion.

Fredericktown was the county seat of Frederick County. In the 1750s, Frederick County was the largest county in Maryland. To the east it started at Georgetown and continued west all the way to Maryland's border with Virginia. (In addition to Frederick, Garrett, Allegany, Washington, Carroll, and Montgomery counties have been carved out of the original Frederick County.) In the 1750s the western boundary was in dispute as was the northern border with Pennsylvania. In fact in the 1730's there was a border war between the two colonies that decided nothing.

Looking east along the creek, about a mile and a half away was Fredericktown. It was a prosperous little town, described by a British officer in April of 1755 as consisting of,

> *"about 200 houses and 2 churches, one English one Dutch the inhabitants, chiefly Dutch are industrious but imposing people."*

Wait a minute. What was a British army officer doing in Frederick in the spring of 1755 and what did that have to do with the building of Schifferstadt? And who are the "Dutch?"

Chapter I Peace and War: 1748-1754

Peace on the Monacacy

By the middle of the 1700s, the English colonies of New York, Pennsylvania, Maryland, and Virginia were all extending settlements west of their original coastal origins. While some of the movement west in Maryland and Virginia was into land no longer occupied or actively claimed by Indian tribes, the efforts of New York and Pennsylvania to claim more land led to disputes with Native tribes. In New York, the Iroquois League of Nations claimed most of the land west of modern day Utica, New York. In Pennsylvania, the Lenape (also known as the Delaware) laid claim to lands from Lancaster County west. During this period, the Quaker government of Pennsylvania perpetrated probably the most notorious land-swindle in North American history.

The Eastern Lenape had agreed to cede some land in northeastern Pennsylvania in accordance with their "Walking Man" tribal law. In essence, the term "Walking Man' meant the distance a non-warrior could cover in a day while walking along a woodland trail – about 30-35 miles. Instead of respecting this law, the colonial government in Philadelphia had woodsmen clear a path through Lenape lands, set up torches for night lighting, and selected a fast runner with good endurance. In addition, to help with training and supplies the runner was offered land incentives for distances beyond the 30-35 mile range. As you can guess, Pennsylvania acquired a piece of land about 100 miles long. As you can also guess, the Lenape quickly acquired extremely bitter feelings about English settlers.

While the English colonies were acquiring lands and settlers were moving west, French explorers and trappers from Canada had been building trading posts along the Ohio River and its tributaries. They became allied with a number of tribes, especially those living in the Ohio Valley, and with the western Pennsylvania Lenape. With English, French and Native tribes all claiming the same land, disputes arose. From about 1715 on, violence flared in the border areas from New York to Virginia. Usually these were localized skirmishes. However, there were two European dynastic wars in the first half of the 1700s that spilled over into North America leading to more widespread raids and massacres.

The negative effect on westward migration of this sporadic warfare was less one might expect. Because of political, religious, and economic repression in Scotland and the Rhineland region of Germany a continuous stream of settlers were ready to take their chances. The allure of cheap land and the chance to make a fresh start overcame the possibility of being burned out or scalped.

In 1748, the Treaty of Aix-la-Chapelle ended the last of these dynastic wars, The War of Austrian Succession, causing hostilities between the British and French and their respective Native American allies in North America to cease. However, no Ohio Valley boundaries were settled. Despite this lack of clarity, English settlers quickly saw the Ohio as their goal. For instance, in 1752 the Ohio Company of Virginia, which included a young George Washington as a shareholder, was granted by King George II 200,000 acres in the Ohio River Valley for settlement. Terms of this land grant required settling 100 families and building a fort within seven years.

With all this western movement, by 1750 residents of Fredericktown probably did not think of it as a frontier town. The Ohio River Valley, which was about 150 miles west, was now the "frontier." If there were future armed conflicts, they most likely would be confined to that area.

Instead, this town founded in 1745 on the western shore of the Monocacy River, had become a colonial agricultural service center for central Frederick County. Agricultural products were either sold locally or taken by wagons east to the Maryland capital of Annapolis for sale or for shipment from the port or north to Lancaster County. In Fredericktown, land now had to be purchased from previous owners and payments and debts were adjudicated in the local court and enforced by a High Sheriff appointed by the Royal Governor.

Also by 1750, Fredericktown was primarily inhabited by German speaking residents from the Upper Rhine valley, some who had been in the "colonies" for at least twenty or thirty years. These people were referred to as Palatines after the name of that region. Most English settlers of the time also referred to all German-speaking immigrants as "Dutch." Mispronouncing the term "Deutsch" probably caused this. Adding to the confusion, many of the Palatines had settled and later sailed from the Netherlands so the term Dutch was applied to them as nationality of origin. During this period there are reports that the German speaking residents felt the English speaking Sheriff was singling them out for unfair treatment.

Typical of 1750-era Fredericktown residents were the Brunners. Joseph Brunner arrived in Philadelphia in 1729 from the Palatine town of Kleine Schifferstadt where he had been a municipal official. By the early 1750s, the Brunner family had acquired four contiguous properties totaling about 1,200 acres from Daniel Dulany. Dulany owned much of what is now Frederick in a parcel of land called Tasker's Chance, named after its previous owner. Joseph Brunner, the family patriarch purchased a 303-acre tract, and named the estate "Shiefferstadt" after their hometown. Joseph's three eldest sons, Henry, John and Jacob, purchased the other three properties. Joseph's youngest son, Elias, probably initially resided with his father on his father's property. In 1753, however, when Elias was thirty years old, Joseph sold "a tract or parcel of Land called "Shiverstadt" [presumably Shiefferstadt] to Elias for 200 pounds.

On the following map, an outline of Tasker's Chance is overlaid on a year 2000 era map of Frederick. The properties A-D are those owned by the Brunners.

Schifferstadt & Brunner Properties in Modern-Day Frederick

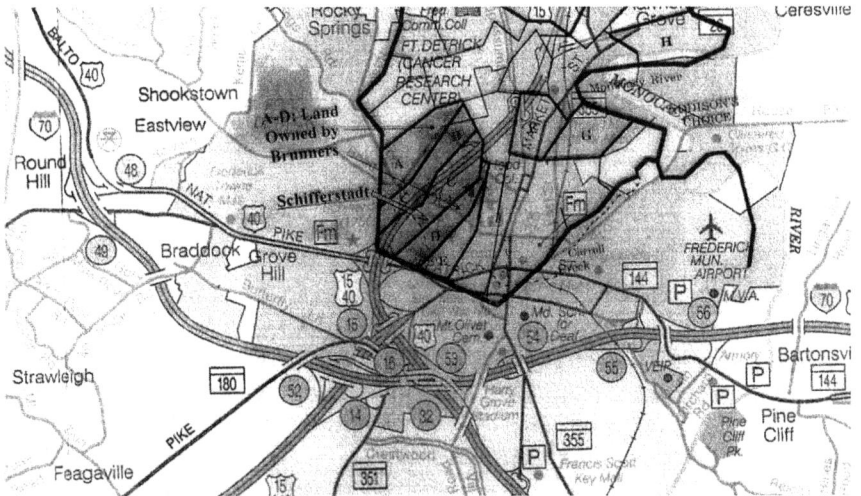

Throughout western Frederick County, Palatines were also settling in fairly large numbers. One of the largest concentrations of Palatines was along Conococheague Creek, about thirty-five miles west of Fredericktown in the Cumberland Valley. In this fertile valley between South and Tuscarora Mountains, the Studebaker, Rench, Hager, and Long families, among others, began to establish farms in the 1740s and

1750s. While some of the families had connections with the Church of the Brethren, the majority attended the Salem German Reformed Church. In addition to the Palatines, a sizable group of Scots were settling in the Pennsylvania portion of the Cumberland Valley. Most of these Scottish settlers were still considered political criminals or terrorists in England (and by many in the royal colonial governments) for their participation in the unsuccessful Jacobite uprising of 1745 that tried to restore "Bonnie Prince Charles" to the throne of England. These people did not accept the legitimacy of the Church of England and were predominantly Presbyterians. By 1755, censuses in western Frederick County and the western Pennsylvania counties just across the border identified thousands of settlers in the Conococheague District.

Crisis On The Ohio: Peace Ends

With the Ohio Company pushing west into lands claimed by both Native American tribes and the French, the relative peacefulness of western Maryland, Virginia, and Pennsylvania was in jeopardy. Added to the lack of specific boundaries were long simmering emotions on both sides that ranged from distrust to hatred. The only open questions were – *When and where would the conflict start?* And, *How widespread would be the fighting?* The answers would be soon, nearby, and from North America, through Europe, and on to India, and the Philippines.

By 1750, France had formally established claims to the Ohio River and its tributaries. Celeron de Blainville led an expedition that marked trees with the French Coat of Arms and buried lead tablets at key eastern points of the French claimed territories. (The Virginia Historical Society in Richmond has the only known surviving plate.)

On June 21 of 1752, Ottowas, Chippewas, and other Ohio tribes under French command attacked Miami (Twightwee) tribes loyal to the British at Pickawillany (near present-day Columbus, Ohio). As a result of this battle, most Ohio tribes pledged their allegiance to the French. In addition, this battle drove Pennsylvania and New York traders from the Ohio River Valley. Throughout 1753, relations between the English colonies and Indian tribes deteriorated. In June of that year, the Mohawk tribe of the Iroquois Nation proclaimed that the "Covenant Chain" (a series of treaties linking Ohio tribes to Iroquois Nations to British colonies) was broken. During the winter of 1753-54, the "Ohio Situation" came to a crisis point. On orders from Virginia Governor Robert Dinwiddie, 21 year-old Major George Washington, accompanied by Christopher Gist, was sent to Ft. Le Boeuf on French Creek (present-day Waterford, Pa) to demand that the French withdraw from the Ohio River Valley. As expected, the French refused. Washington returned quickly to Williamsburg, despite numerous hardships and a near drowning in an ice-strewn river, and published his account: *The Journal of Major George Washington Sent By The Hon. Robert Dinwiddie, Esq; His Majesty's Lieutenant-Governor, and Commander in Chief of Virginia, To The Commandant of the French Forces on Ohio*.

It quickly became a best seller in the colonies, especially Virginia, Pennsylvania, and Massachusetts. Public opinion started to call for action on the Ohio frontier.

In response to the French, Virginia Governor Dinwiddie approved the Ohio Company plan to begin building a fort at the Forks of the Ohio (present-day Pittsburgh). In addition, Dinwiddie also ordered a Royal Colonial Regiment and Virginia militia to re-enforce the fort. These troops also began construction of a military road from Wills Creek (Cumberland, Md) to the Forks of the Ohio. (Much of US 40 follows this road.)

Major George Washington was second in command of this expedition. However, when the commander, Colonel Joshua Frey died after an accident in late May, Washington assumed command as the column moved west from Wills Creek. When Washington reached Redstone Creek, near present-day Uniontown, Pa, in May 1754 he encountered Virginia militia led by an Ensign Ward retreating from the Forks of the Ohio. They had been driven out of the uncompleted fort on April 17, 1754 by a large force of French and Canadians. French forces built a new and stronger fort at the Forks and named it Ft. Duquesne for the French Governor-General of Canada.

Ft. Duquesne, Forks of the Ohio, Pittsburgh, Pa
Stones Outline the French Fort

Washington established camp at a clearing east of Laurel Mountain called "The Great Meadows" and considered his options.

The events of the next three months of 1754 are the subject of many books and articles and are still controversial. The following is just a quick summary.

At about 7:00 am on May 28, 1754, after receiving reports from his Seneca allies that a French scouting party was sent from Ft. Duquesne to intercept his force, Washington led a force of about 40 Virginians and Seneca to intercept them. Washington had decided that their intention was similar to his, scouting and probing the enemy's position, and not diplomatic in nature. He also apparently felt that the French actions at the Forks constituted an act of war and therefore, hostilities between the English and French had already begun. In the early morning, a French force of about 33 soldiers was discovered camped in a glen on the eastern slope of Laurel Mountain. Washington quietly surrounded the camp with his troops. What happened next is still open to debate. The French maintained that Washington's force fired first despite the French attempt to "parlay" with him. The English response was that

Washington's force only fired in response.

Jumonville Glen, Pa
Site of the French Camp

The ambush lasted fifteen minutes. Only one Frenchman escaped. The French commander, Ensign Joseph Coulon de Villiers Jumonville was wounded and captured. He was then turned over to the Seneca chief "Half King" who killed him.

> *This 15-minute skirmish at "Jumonville Glen" sets off a worldwide struggle for empire that will last 9 years. It will be called the Seven Years War and has been called the First World War by historians. Battles will be fought in North America, the Caribbean, India, and the Philippines. Massive land battles will be fought on the European continent with over 100,000 soldiers engaged. Thousands of soldiers and civilians will be killed. The British Empire will be established and the seeds for the fall of the French Monarchy will be planted. It will lead directly to the American Revolution.*

The escaped French soldier reached Ft. Duquesne and reported the massacre. A French officer at the fort, Louis Coulon de Villiers, Joseph's half-brother, swore revenge on Washington for "assassinating" him. He assembled a force of about 600-700 French and Indians and quickly marched east from Ft. Duquesne. Reports of the "assassination" were sent to Quebec and forwarded to Paris along with calls for war on the English.

In anticipation of the coming attack, Washington dug in at Great Meadows, which is about 5 miles east of "Jumonville Glen" along present-day US 40. He called the fortification "Fort Necessity." About 400 re-enforcements arrived from Wills Creek. Even with these re-enforcements, Washington was outnumbered. Furthermore, Ft. Necessity was located on marshy ground between two creeks and was surrounded by wooded hills that would give an attacking force cover.

It might appear that the "prudent" course of action would have been to retire to Wills Creek and offer battle at that stronger position. However, the combination of the single-minded English objective of occupying the Forks of the Ohio, the 18th Century concept of military honor, and Washington's overwhelming self-confidence meant that retreat without a battle was not possible.

While Washington and his forces awaited battle, an Interprovincial Congress was meeting at Albany in June to attempt a reconstruction of the Covenant Chain. This series of daylong meetings was held at the estate of William Johnson who for many years had conducted diplomatic relations between the English and the Native Tribes. Despite the best intentions of Johnson and others, disputes between New York and Pennsylvania arose which prevented meaningful agreements. By early July, Native Indian tribes began to leave the Congress and began to deliberate their choice of future alliances - French or British.

Reconstructed Ft. Necessity: The Great Meadows, Pa
The French and Indian attackers occupied the tree line
above and around the fort.
Note the shallow trench line around the stockade.

On July 3, 1754, French and Indian forces arrived at Great Meadows and refused to fight Washington's troops that had formed ranks in conventional 18th Century military style on the flat, open Great Meadows. Instead, they filed into the surrounding woods and began firing their muskets from hidden positions. They continued shooting all day. A heavy rain filled the trenches of Ft. Necessity and drenched their powder. Washington's troops took heavy casualties, but Washington refused to ask for terms. At 8:00 pm, despite having suffered only one fatality, but fearing possible English re-enforcements, Coulon de Villiers offered terms.

In the early morning of July 4th Washington signed a document that allowed his troops to march to Wills Creek with their firearms and possessions. A much-disputed section of the surrender document, however, stated that Washington was personally responsible for the "assassination" of Jumonville. Washington said repeatedly that the document was blurred by rain and wasn't translated properly to him. Furthermore, Washington did not consider the "Jumonville Affair" as initiating any conflict with the French or a personal assault and instead saw it as a necessary military response to the earlier French capture of the Ohio Company fort at the Forks of the Ohio. The debate rages to this day.

By the fall of 1754 news of Washington's defeat reached London. The British government saw this defeat as a major setback to its North American strategy and proposed a significant response. Major General Edward Braddock was appointed commander of North American forces and two British regiments were ordered to North America to capture Ft. Duquesne and other French fortifications. Braddock and the regiments arrived in Alexandria, Virginia in late March 1755. The English Board of Trade, which ran the commerce of the colonies, authorized extra taxes on the American colonies to finance Braddock's expedition and also authorized Massachusetts' governor Shirley to raise colonial troops.

Despite Washington's defeat and the retreat of troops from the frontier, French and Indian attacks on western settlers were minimal for the rest of 1754 and into the spring of 1755.

Thoughts of defending their own property from Indian attacks were probably not on the minds of the Brunners or other residents of Fredericktown or for that manner on the minds of settlers along Conococheague Creek in early 1755. In fact, thoughts of a quick victory over the French and their Indian allies were the more probable sentiments. After all, the summer of 1755 would see two British regiments composed of tough veterans of many European campaigns and a full train of artillery marching west to give battle. Surely the much smaller French force and their "unreliable" tribal warrior allies could not stand up to such a force.

Chapter II Braddock's Defeat: 1755

Dunbar's Regiment Comes to Fredericktown

On April 18th, 1755, about one-half of Braddock's army reached Fredericktown. This was Thomas Dunbar's regiment (the 48th) of British regulars, Virginia recruits, and assorted camp followers. All totaled, they numbered about 900-1,000. In addition, about thirty English sailors also arrived with Dunbar. They had been detached from British warships at Alexandria to assist with the artillery.

The arrival of these troops doubled the population of Fredericktown overnight.

And this brings us back to the observation of the British officer with Dunbar's force.

> *"This town has not been settled above 7 years and there are about 200 houses and 2 churches, one English one Dutch [German Reformed Church] the inhabitants, chiefly Dutch [German] are industrious but imposing [take unfair advantage of] people: here we got plenty of provisions and forage."*

Besides the attitude of the inhabitants, the British commander was also met with two unexpected and unwelcomed surprises.

First, despite the promises that Maryland governor Horatio Sharpe had given earlier in the year at a war conference conducted at the Carlyle House in Alexandria, there was no road west from Fredericktown to Wills Creek (the route of I-70 and I-68), where Dunbar's troops were to meet the remainder of Braddock's forces coming from Alexandria. This meant that his force would have to detour south, crossing the Potomac River at the Mouth of the Conococheague (Williamsport, Md.) and proceed west through what is now West Virginia and recross the Potomac River at Old Town, which is about twenty miles east of Wills Creek. This detour would cost the expedition at least a week.

Second, and more alarming, was that the wagons and supplies promised by Sharpe, and the primary reason half of Braddock's army was sent through Maryland, were not in Frederick.

To say the least, Fredericktown would be the center of a full-scale political and military brouhaha that April of 1755.

General Braddock and his staff arrived on April 21st and gave orders to round up all available livestock and enlist (draft or conscript seems a more accurate description) wagon drivers. Daniel Dulany Jr., son of the owner of Tasker's Chance, reported the effects of this order:

> "Soon after the General's arrival at Frederick Town, orders were issued to recruiting officers to enlist all able-bodied men, servants not excepted. These orders were punctually executed by the officers of Dunbar's Regiment, to the great injury and oppression of many poor people, whose livelihood depended in great measure upon their property in their servants."

One wonders if Dulany's definition of "poor people" meant something like "put-upon" since it seems they had enough resources to either retain indentured servants or own slaves, which the term servant also meant.

Shortly thereafter Governor Sharpe arrived and tried to negotiate a solution. This resulted in an unsatisfactory compromise that would make Fredericktown wagons and drivers available for only the thirty-some mile stretch to the Potomac River crossing. This short distance was virtually useless to the campaign.

It was only the arrival of Benjamin Franklin, appointed by the Pennsylvania legislature as Postmaster General for the colony, which allowed the expedition to continue west. He procured wagons, horses, drivers, and cattle from nearby Pennsylvania farms by insuring their return on his personal assets. Some of these wagons proceeded directly to Fredericktown while others traveled south on what it now US 11, passing along the western side of Conococheague Creek and continued to the Potomac River to rendezvous with the British at what is now Williamsport, Maryland.

Did the Brunners have any contacts with the British or Colonial troops? Especially those sent to round up livestock and drivers? While no written records have been found, the proximity of the Brunner properties and the military camps makes it highly likely.

Proposed Location of Dunbar's 48th Regimental, Colonial Infantry, British Artillery, and Wagon Camps: Frederick, Maryland April 1755
(See Appendix I for Details on Camp Location)

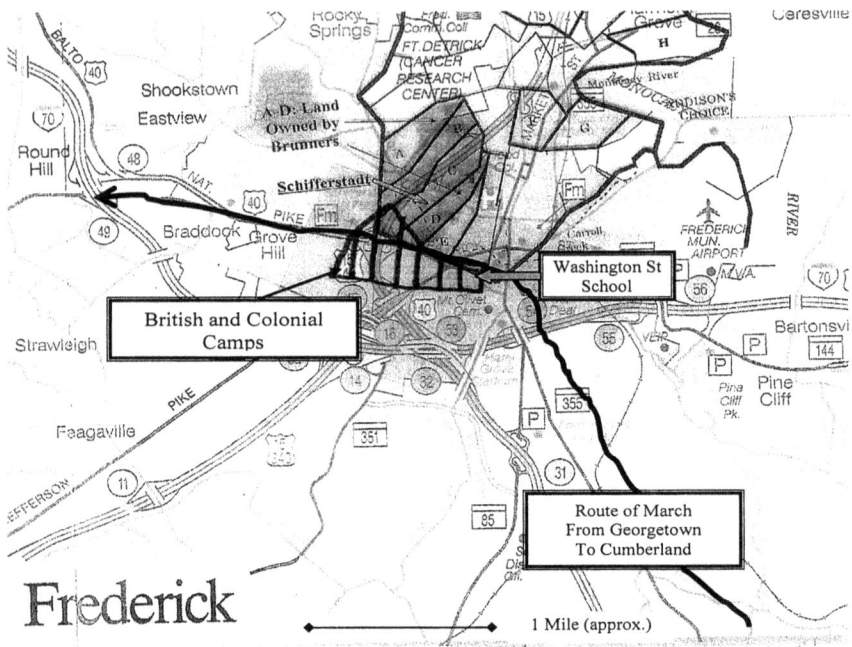

Frederick

1 Mile (approx.)

With no evidence to the contrary, it's safe to assume that the Brunners went along with the rest of the Fredericktown residents and refused to sell their livestock (at below market prices) to the British army or allow their wagons or servants be drafted into the campaign. It is also probably safe to assume that the Brunners were either among those "*many poor people, whose livelihood depended in great measure upon their property in their servants*" that Dulany referred to or were their neighbors. It is also probably safe to conclude that relations between the English speaking troops, especially the officers, and the German-speaking residents were frayed to say the least.

Finally, by April 29, 1755, Dunbar's troops were marching west over Catoctin Mountain and back to Virginia. Braddock, accompanied by his new unpaid aide-de-camp George Washington, who had arrived in Fredericktown amidst the turmoil, followed the next day. Left behind were the horses, wagons, and servants of the residents, and what appears to be an overwhelmingly negative impression of the Fredericktown Palatinate settlers in the minds of Franklin ("Palatinate boors"), Washington, and the English officers. One could almost hear them saying they never wanted to pass through Frederick again. And one could almost hear the Fredericktown residents say something similar about them ever passing through again. Of course, no one at the time thought these ill-feelings would have any long term effects because, with or without Fredericktown, Braddock was sure to be on the road to victory.

Defeat on The Monongahela

In the *Germania,* the Roman historian Tacitus writes of a Roman general Varius who in the summer of AD 9 led his proud legions into the Teutoburger forest of what is now Germany without having any knowledge of how the German tribes conducted deep woodland guerilla warfare. Furthermore, since he had absolutely no respect for his adversary he didn't bother to try to learn. Finally, he took his heavily equipped legions far beyond their normal supply lines. His troops were surrounded and massacred. In 1976 the German artist Anselm Kiefer produced an amazing painting that in abstract form captures the horrors of that battle.

On July 9, 1755, English General Edward Braddock came very close to repeating that history.

The summer was spent slowly pushing over the Allegheny ridges and improving the road Washington started a year earlier. Due to his frustration with the slow pace, Braddock accepted Washington's recommendation that a smaller, faster column be used to attack the fort. A main camp (Dunbar's Camp) was established just north of Jumonville Glen. Most of Dunbar's 48th regiment remained at the camp with the heavy artillery, supplies, and the hospital. Braddock took a "flying column" composed of parts of the 44th and the 48th, a naval detachment with several cannons, and colonial troops north to Ft. Duquesne.

A restored section of Braddock's Road near Jumonville, Pa
This is very similar to what "Braddocks's Field" looked like on
July 9th 1755.

At first all went well. In fact, the sight of this column demoralized the Indians at the Fort and many decided to return to their villages west in the Ohio country. But, just as Braddock's troops prepared to cross the Monongahela, French re-enforcements arrived at Ft. Duquesne and a French Captain Beaujeu successfully rallied the Indian warriors. Braddock completed a complex double crossing of the Monongahela without incident and the advanced guard marched about two more miles before they collided with the onrushing French at 1 o'clock in the afternoon. They were about eight miles short of Ft. Duquesne.

The French commander Beaujeu was killed instantly by British gunfire but the predominantly Indian force looped around both flanks of the British force and began laying down heavy musket fire. Using the heavy woods and ravines for cover they gained the advantage and would keep it all afternoon. Advancing British and Colonial troops ran into units no longer able to advance and troops from the lead section fell back causing all units to lose their formations. The wagon train turned around and bolted back across the river. Among the drivers was Daniel Boone.

The British lines lost all order and British officers were quickly falling. For three long hours the battle went on. Braddock was wounded and fell. All the other British officers were either killed or wounded. Only Washington, who was still suffering from the effects of a fever, remained unwounded and took command. Fortunately, for the British, the Indians are unable to completely cut off the road back to the river. Washington gathered up the survivors and fought a rear-guard action, allowing a safe crossing of the Monongahela. Of the 1,400 British and Colonial troops who made it to "Braddock's Field" that day, about 450 were killed and another 420 wounded. Only one-third of the "flying column" escaped physically intact.

Braddock's Field Today: Braddock, Pa

Approximately 500-600 Indian warriors, and 50-100 French-Canadian rangers attacked that day. Fewer than fifty were killed or wounded. Many were veterans of earlier battles including the 1752 attack at Pickawillany. Others such as Pontiac would become leaders in later battles and wars. Although they were outnumbered nearly two to one, they won by using superior tactics and making better use of the terrain. More important than just winning the battle, they changed the entire strategic situation in the British North American colonies. By the end of the year Fredericktown residents would know first-hand what this defeat meant.

Washington was able to lead the demoralized survivors to Dunbar's Camp at Jumonville Glen. The Indians did not pursue. They stayed on the field of battle and scalped and mutilated the dead and wounded left on the field but did not bury the remains. They also collected the arms and supplies left on the field. Hundreds of muskets, thirteen cannons and mortars, and extensive supplies of gunpowder and bullets were taken back to Ft. Duquesne for later use.

When the survivors reached Dunbar's Camp a panic took over, probably helped along by the death of Braddock. Vast quantities of supplies, over 150 wagons full, were either burned or buried to free up the remaining horses and wagons to carry the wounded as the hurried retreat to Wills Creek began.

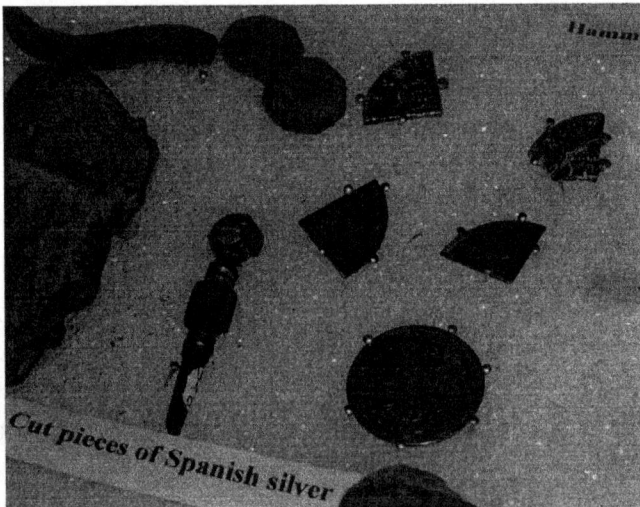

Spanish Silver Coin "Quartered" to Make Change by British Troops
Found at "Dunbar's Camp"

20

Washington buried Braddock near Ft. Necessity under the recently built road and ran wagons over it so his body would not be found by French or Indian war parties. He was able to keep the retreat from turning into a route but just barely.

Washington left the wreckage of the British force at Wills Creek. He returned to Williamsburg, Virginia totally disgusted with British military ability. His solid, courageous performance restored his reputation and he was shortly given command of the Virginia frontier (April 5, 1756), but given pitifully few troops to defend it.

By late summer of 1755 British troops continued their retreat eastward from Wills Creek leaving only a few Virginia militia at Ft. Cumberland to protect the frontier. They retraced their path eastward through Virginia and re-crossed the Potomac at Conococheague (Willimasport, Md). They continued up present day US 11 and camped for several days near Greencastle, Pa before proceeding to Carlisle, Pa.

At this point, the surviving British officers had a choice of two paths. They could either turn east toward Fredericktown and then proceed to Carlisle or continue directly north (following US 11) to Carlisle. Even though the road from Fredericktown to Carlisle was probably safer because South Mountain served as protection on the west, and Fredericktown would have offered the chance to resupply the survivors, probably remembered their stay in Fredericktown, marched directly to Carlisle. They didn't stop for long anywhere but continued on to Philadelphia where they went into "winter quarters" in September.

While the remnants of the 44th and 48th regiments went north, civilians that accompanied Braddock's forces continued east to Fredericktown. It was the closest town to the frontier and would possibly offer shelter and a chance to recover from their wounds and fevers.

We know something about these times from the diary of Charlotte Browne. Mrs. Browne, as she was referred to, came with Braddock's forces from England in 1755. She served as a surgeon's assistant with the 44th Regiment. Charlotte's brother, a British army officer contracted a fever on the march and died at Ft. Cumberland. Charlotte had stayed with her brother and therefore (and fortunately for her) did not accompany the expedition to Dunbar's Camp or Braddock's Field.

On August 20, 1755, Charlotte Browne began the retreat from Ft.

Cumberland back through Virginia. After being thrown off a horse and nearly killed, as well as getting lost several times, she arrived in Frederick on August 30. Ten days to travel about ninety miles. She writes that she stayed with a "Widow DeButts" in Fredericktown.

On September 10, 1755, she took a walk through Frederick and reported that it was, *"a very pleasant place most of the people are Dutch* [German speaking Palatines]."Five days later, she received an invitation to meet *"all the English ladies in the Town,"* and on September 20, 1755; Mrs. Browne attended a Ball *"composed of Romans, Jews, and Hereticks [non-Anglican Protestants] who in this town flock together. The ladies danced without stays or Hoops."*

Note that Mrs. Browne reported that the English and German populations did not mingle socially.

While Charlotte and other survivors were recovering in Fredericktown, French commanders and Indian leaders were beginning a major offensive in western Maryland and Pennsylvania.

Chapter III Total War on the Frontier

The Indian and French Plan

With the survivors from Braddock's expedition safely in camp near Philadelphia, English and German settlers in western Pennsylvania, Maryland and Virginia were virtually without protection.

The Indian tribes that participated in the Battle of the Monongahela, primarily the Shawanoe and the Lenape, saw this as an opportunity to correct a century's worth of wrongdoing and illegal land purchases by the English colonies and the white settlers. For once, they had the military advantage, including more and better weaponry to completely remove all white settlements from the Ohio Valley to east of the last Appalachian ridge.

The French saw a military advantage in this strategy as well. By laying waste to such a large swath of land and creating a refugee crisis in the Mid-Atlantic colonies, the English government would be forced to commit soldiers that would otherwise be used to attack the French capital of Quebec or other French possessions in North America. Furthermore, this plan could be accomplished with a relatively small number of French and Canadian soldiers.

The attacks on the settlements would be different this time. They would be planned, coordinated, thorough, and well-supported. The Lenape village of Kittanning on the Allegheny River (present-day Kittanning, Pa) became the "command-and control center" of this campaign. It was located on several important Indian trails that led to all of the white settlements. Large quantities of weapons and ammunition were stockpiled there. Quarters for captured settlers were built. It was here that French "advisors" and Tribal chiefs planned the attacks and organized the war parties and logistics necessary for their success.

Parnell's Knob in the Cumberland Valley
Its distinctive shape was used by war-parties as guidance to and from
Kittanning

The tactics would be simple, the complete destruction of all settlements. All buildings: houses, barns, mills, workshops, and outbuildings would be burnt. All livestock would be killed and all crops destroyed. Male settlers and militia would be scalped and killed. Women and children would, if possible, be captured.

The campaign started in the autumn of 1755. By October, Charlotte Browne was writing about it.

> October 7, 1755: *"An express [mail] from Cumberland reports that 5 families have been scalped, only 3 days of bread remain."*

> October 8, 1755: Another express from Cumberland *"begs some assistance,"* according to Mrs. Browne.

Two days later, Charlotte Browne left for Philadelphia to rejoin the British troops.

On November 1, 1755, the largest attack thus far took place. An Indian and French raiding party attacked the settlement at Great Cove (near present-day McConnellsburg, Pa). It was completely destroyed and members of 47 out of 93 families were either killed or captured. By the end of December 1755 many settlements in western Pennsylvania, Maryland and Virginia were abandoned. In Pennsylvania alone an estimated 500 whites were killed, wounded, or captured.

This first phase of the campaign essentially drove out the majority of white settlements west of the Cumberland Valley. All that remained in Maryland was the small garrison at Ft. Cumberland, some part-time militia commanded by Colonel Cressap at Old Town along the Potomac River, and a small wooden fort at Stoddert's (Hancock, Md). In western Pennsylvania, the situation was somewhat better with approximately 24 private and 10 Provincial forts and a small number of militia units.

These attacks were treated as a major catastrophe. In late 1755 George Washington declared that in unless something was done, *"there would not be fifteen families left in Frederick County."* Maryland Governor Sharpe added, *"all land beyond Fredericktown would soon be abandoned."*

As the winter of 1755-1756 set in, Fredericktown was becoming a refugee center for settlers from western Maryland and Pennsylvania. However, since the villages and settlements in the Cumberland Valley just west of South Mountain had not been attacked and several additional forts were being built by the settlers along Conococheague Creek, the threat of attacks did not yet seem imminent in Fredericktown. The "frontier" was still west of Tuscarora Mountain, some forty or so miles away.

1756: Fire on The Conococheague

The French and Indian campaign to remove white settlements came to the Cumberland Valley with a calculated swiftness in the late winter and early spring of 1756. In the Conococheague District alone, attacks are reported on February 11th and 29th, March 1st and 3rd, and April 1st. Settlers were killed or captured, farms burnt and two stockaded private forts, Ft. McCord and Ft. David Davis were overrun.

The local militia quickly discovered just how well organized these attacks were. During the attack on McDowell's Mills, (March 1st) the combined Indian and French war-party used European style tactics to outflank and out maneuver the defenders rather than using the guerilla style hit-and-run tactics the defenders were expecting.

The Pennsylvania militia pursued the Conococheague attackers but were badly defeated. According to an April 15, 1756 report published in the

Pennsylvania Gazette, the battle took place near Sideling Hill and the militia was driven back with heavy casualties. It is reported that only 25 of the 50 soldiers returned.

Cumberland Valley looking west toward Tuscarora Mt.
Farms and forts attacked in early 1756 were near the silos in the middle distance. In summer 1756 this view would have shown a wasteland of burnt buildings and crops.

On the same day, the Maryland Gazette reported that Virginia soldiers under Washington's command at Ft. Cumberland,

> *"lately met with some Indians and a French Officer, and took off his Scalp, and found upon him some Cloths that belonged to Lieutenant Bacon (who was kill'd in the Engagement within 4 miles of Ft. Cumberland and a Scalp suppos'd to be Mr. Bacon's.)"*

The Maryland Gazette also carried a report on refugees from the Conococheague attacks. The April 29, 1756 edition stated that,

> *"Last Saturday there came to Baltimore Town, from Conococheague, at the Foot of the North Mountain, 41 Persons, viz. 6 Men, 5 Women, and 30 Children, with some of their cattle to avoid the Fury of the Enemy."*

Meanwhile on May 17th in Europe, France and England formally declared war on each other. This was nearly two years after Jumonville Glen and four years after Pickawillany. While this declaration set off hostilities in Europe, it made no difference in North America. Countless battles, skirmishes, and massacres had already been fought and would continue to be fought.

Marking Maryland's first response to the crisis on its western border, Governor Horatio Sharpe departed Annapolis for the frontier on June 3rd. The purpose of this trip was to oversee the construction of a large stone fort of classic European design, Ft. Frederick, located near the Potomac River at Big Pool, Md. This is about midway between Conococheague Creek and Stoddert's Fort (Hancock, Md). The Maryland legislature had appropriated some money for the fort, but not enough to build it quickly and not enough to garrison it. In fact the 1756 session of the legislature did not approve any money to pay for a frontier militia.

Also, in news from the New York Mercury, it was reported that Colonel Daniel Webb had arrived from London to take command of the 48th regiment, "late Colonel Dunbar's."

Attacks in Maryland and Pennsylvania continued. In June a large party of reapers in Maryland near the Conococheague were attacked. It was reported that all were killed or captured. The Ft. Frederick construction project, about ten miles away, had no effect.

On July 24th 1756, the French commander of Ft. Duquesne was able to write to Paris of the success of their strategy.

> "It is by means such as I have mentioned, varied in every form to suit the occasion, that I have succeeded in ruining the three adjacent provinces, Pennsylvania, Maryland, and Virginia, driving off the inhabitants and totally destroying the settlements over a tract of country thirty leagues wide [approximately 82 miles] reckoning from the line of Ft. Cumberland. M. de Contrecoeur [previous commander of Ft. Duquesne] had not gone a week before I had six or seven different war-parties in the field at once, accompanied by Frenchmen. Thus far, we have lost only two officers and a few soldiers; but the Indian villages are full of prisoners of every age and sex.

The enemy has lost far more since the battle [Braddock's defeat] than on the day of his defeat."

Approximately eighty-two miles east from Ft. Cumberland is Hagerstown, Md. This report indicated that the Cumberland Valley was fairly well destroyed. It would be virtually abandoned by the end of summer.

On July 30th a fatal blow was struck at Ft. Granville (present-day Lewistown, Pa). The capture and destruction of this provincial fort (built and garrisoned by the government of Pennsylvania) caused the flight from the valley of about 80 percent of the population. In addition, all forts except Ft. Littleton were abandoned. It was reported that after the assault only 100 men who could bear arms remained in the region. Before the attacks began in 1756, there were reported to be 3,000.

The last major attack of the summer occurred near the mouth of the Conococheague on the Potomac (Williamsport, Md) on August 27th when a predominately Palatinate settlement was attacked. Thirty-nine people were reported killed and many more wounded or captured.
Governor Sharpe referred to this attack as:

> *"Thence they (party of Indians) made a Descent into this Province [from Pennsylvania] and cut off some People that lived more than twelve on this side our Fort [Fort Frederick]. This Accident has so terrified our Back Inhabitants that Hundreds of them have abandoned their plantations and one our most flourishing German Settlements is on the Brink of being entirely broke up..."*

Washington also had received reports on the effects of these attacks in the Cumberland Valley,

> *"transmitted to me by several hands, and confirmed yesterday by Henry Brinker, who left Monocacy [near Frederick] the day before, and who also affirms that three hundred and fifty wagons had passed that place, to avoid the enemy, within the space of three days."*

The site of the August 27th attack on the Palatine settlement was within thirty miles of Fredericktown. It was also where Colonel Dunbar and his troops, marching west from Fredericktown, and confident of victory, had crossed into Virginia only sixteen months earlier.

It was now the frontline of the Seven Years War.

The View From Fredericktown

Looking out from a house in Fredericktown that September must have been bleak, for the sight of over one hundred wagons heading east in one day and with wounded survivors telling of losing husbands or wives, or sons, or daughters, would have been almost too much to bear. Indian attacks through the gaps in the mountains were expected daily and no soldiers were seen arriving from the east to take up the fight.

Indian Attacks within 50 Miles of Schifferstadt
July 1755-April 1758

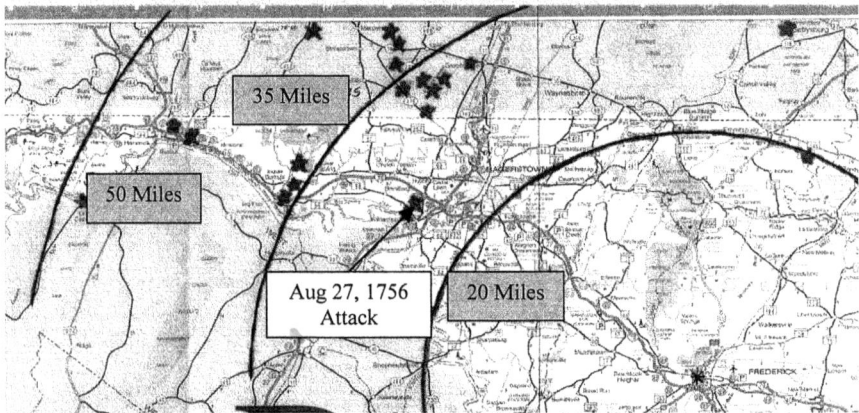

35 Miles

50 Miles

Aug 27, 1756
Attack

20 Miles

Sources: Maryland Gazette, Conococheague Institute, Calvin Bricker, Jr.

As autumn came to the Monocacy valley in 1756 it seemed likely that it would be Fredericktown's turn under the knife in the coming year. Residents looking at maps of the period would have plotted out the location of many of the attacks, and as this map displays, seen how close the August 27th attack at the Mouth of the Conococheague was to the town. With Indian and French war parties able to travel fifty or more miles per day, it must have seen too close for much comfort. (Appendix II contains a list of the attacks depicted on this map.)

For the Palatine immigrants living in Fredericktown the seriousness of the situation also presented a dilemma as to what they should do. The majority of the Palatines that settled throughout the English colonies had come to North America to escape either religious persecution or the outright destruction of their villages in religious wars. Their beliefs on the war ranged from non-involvement; it was a war between the English,

French, and Indians, they wanted no part of it, to a religious based pacifism that believed no war was justified.

Therefore, while they had agreed to settle on the western fringes of the colonies despite possible dangers, they had hoped they could escape being involved in any future wars. In many ways they were trying to carve out a separate existence from the people around them. Perhaps an Indian speaker at a conference in Quebec in 1756, said it best, *"a Nation which is neither French nor English, nor Indian, and inhabits the lands around us."*

In Maryland, the opinion of the English colonial government wasn't as benign. In 1751, three years before hostilities began; the Maryland Committee of Grievances and Courts of Justice issued the following statement:

> *"That as the Numbers of Germans, French, and other Foreigners come into and settle the back and remote Parts, among which are divers Papists and Jesuits, or Priests of their own Nations, will, if not timely prevented, all together become a dangerous intestine enemy, ready to join French or Indians, who are but too near, and surrounding the British Settlements on this Continent,"*

From available records though, we can see what some of the German-speaking residents of Fredericktown did that winter. Despite criticism of their religious beliefs and the refusal of many to join in the active defense of Maryland, they stayed. Not only did they stay, but they also took in their Palatinate kinsmen from the Conococheague and elsewhere during this critical period.

Chapter IV "Shelter From the Storm"

The Maryland Room of the C. Burr Artz Library in Frederick contains the 18th century records of the two Fredericktown churches mentioned by the 1755 chronicler from the 48th regiment. These churches were the German Reformed Church of Fredericktown (German Palatines) and the All Saints Anglican Church (National Church of England). Records of the christenings from both churches show a very interesting pattern from 1755 to 1760. Since both churches christened children shortly after birth, these records are good surrogates for the number of births that occurred during that period.

Seven Years War Fredericktown Christenings
German Reformed and All Saints Churches

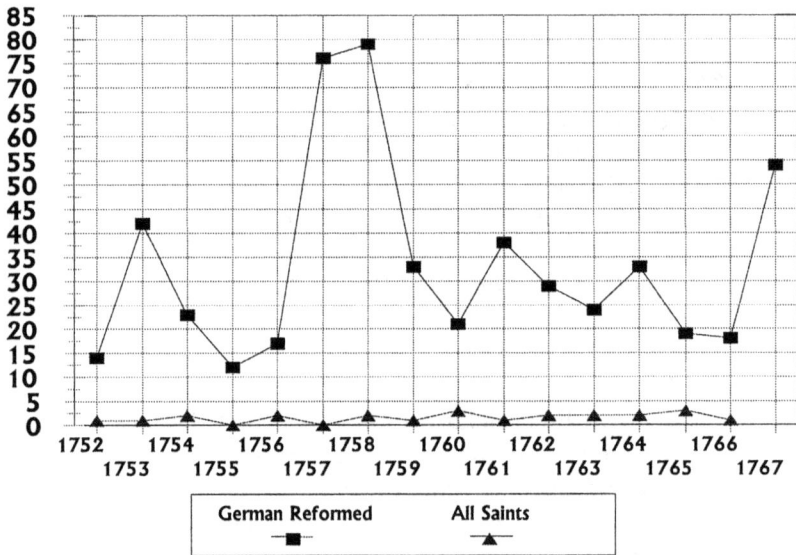

The key numbers in this graph are the German Reformed christenings for the years 1757 and 1758. Look what happens right after the Cumberland Valley and the Palatine settlements in the Conococheague District are abandoned. There was over a four-fold increase in number of christenings recorded at the Frederick Reformed Church from 1756 to 1757 - from 17 to 76. This number stayed about the same in 1758 and then fell back to near pre-war rates by 1760.

This increase is so rapid and so large that it cannot be simply explained by more pregnancies occurring in the existing population. Instead, such a dramatic increase reflects a large increase in the population of Fredericktown during those critical years.

This conclusion is based on the following.

As for potential births, in 1756 there were at most 200 German Reformed families in the Fredericktown Church. (In 1756 there were approximately 200 houses in the town and about 80 percent of the population was estimated to actively belong to that church.) To produce approximately 80 live births a year for two years in a row from this population would have required every woman of child bearing age to have a child two years in a row. That is highly unlikely. Simply put, there would not be enough healthy and fertile women to have that many successful pregnancies. The reality of these conditions are reflected in the more consistent birthrates in the years other than 1757 and 1758 and in the All Saints christening information that showed no significant changes during 1757 or 1758.

Instead, what seems clear is that many of the people who sought refuge in Fredericktown were the Palatine settlers from Conococheague, some of whom were probably members of the Salem German Reformed community near Welsh Run, Pennsylvania. Adding to the connection between these two settlements, Theodore Frankenfeld was, until his death in 1756, the pastor for Reformed congregations in both Fredericktown and Conococheague.

We also know from the records of the Fredericktown Reformed Church that the Brunners were members of the Fredericktown Reformed congregation.

In 1753 four Brunners received Confirmation and Anna Maria, daughter of Henry and Magdalena Brunner, was christened on January 18, 1753. In 1754 two additional family members, Catherine and Anna Mary received Confirmation as well. A list of communicants for Easter, 1758 included two Johns and a Jacob Brunner. One John and Jacob were sons of Joseph. The other John was probably a grandson of Joseph (see below). An undated page from the period of 1758-59 lists a Henry Brunner and a John Brunner both passing their catechumen at the age of 14 and a Catherine Brunner passing hers at the age of 13. In addition, a Maria Elois Brunner is recorded as marrying a John Mittalraul on July 19, 1757 and a Jacob Brunner married Maria Barbara Kaufer on April 1, 1759.

The other question that comes from looking at this graph is why there wasn't a similar increase in christening at All Saints Church? There is a simple answer. Virtually none of the refugees were members of the Anglican Church.

Why? In addition to the Palatine settlers in the Cumberland Valley, the other major group of settlers was Scottish. As mentioned earlier, these Scottish settlers had come to America to escape persecution because of their participation in the unsuccessful Jacobite uprising of 1745 that tried to restore "Bonnie Prince Charles" as King of England. These people did not accept the legitimacy of the Church of England and were predominantly Presbyterians.

Hence, they would not be taking communion at All Saints Church nor would they be welcomed in many of the English homes of Fredericktown. However, they also would not be members of the German Reformed Church. So, while marriages between Palatine and Scottish settlers in the Cumberland Valley are recorded, it is hard to say with any certainty how many Scottish settlers took shelter in Fredericktown. We do know that some Scotts remained in the Cumberland Valley in late 1756 and that they participated in one of the boldest raids of the Seven Years War.

So, it appears that immigrants from the Palatinate, now living in Fredericktown, showed their Christian faith by helping their fellow man. They provided "Shelter From The Storm."

How Many People Took Shelter in Fredericktown?

Trying to extrapolate the actual number of people that took refuge in Fredericktown from the christening numbers is tricky. However, by assuming the same family size for the refugees as for the Fredericktown residents and the same birth rate, about 2.2 births per one-hundred people, it appears that over 2,500 people could have taken refuge each of the two years. This number represents the population of the families that would have had the additional sixty babies recorded in both 1757 and 1758. The following table shows how this estimate was derived.

Possible Refugee Population
Fredericktown 1757-1758

	Annual Births (avg.)	Population @ 2.2 births per 100 people
Pre-1757	18	800
1757-58 Total	78	3,500
1757-58 Refugee Population	78-18= 60	3,500-800= 2,700

This number, while seemingly high, is not an unreasonable estimate. Calvin Bricker, a Greencastle, Pennsylvania historian of the Conococheague region, has estimated that approximately 5,000 people lived in that region prior to the attacks. He also estimates that approximately 400 people from the region were killed or wounded during the attacks. This would mean that upwards of 4,500 people might have abandoned the region. 2,700 is about sixty percent of that number. From genealogies of the Conococheague region, it is not unreasonable to assume that about that many were Palatines. So, while that number does seem high, the christening data does support it.

At the other end of the scale, a low-end estimate could be based on only pregnant women, young children, and others suffering from illness or wounds staying in Fredericktown while more able-bodied people continued on to find refuge elsewhere. Using this approach, an estimate of about 400 to 500 people would be obtained.

Most likely, the actual number was somewhere in between these estimates and probably did vary depending on the season with the winter numbers being higher. (During farming season some refugees might have traveled to work on farms throughout central Maryland.)

The answer to why the number of christenings fell so dramatically after 1758 will be coming in a later chapter.

Where Did They Stay?

Where Did They Stay?

We know one response. The extended Brunner family built a 30^{ft} by 40^{ft} fieldstone "fortified house." Confronted with the realities of impending attacks, providing shelter for kinsmen who had been burned out of their houses, little immediate help from the English authorities, and a religious position that ruled out offensive action, a very large, very strong defensive structure was the only immediate solution. A wood frame house, a style that was becoming popular in the Mid-Atlantic colonies because of its ease of construction and low cost to heat, would be too easily burnt if attacked. A log house was somewhat more stout, but as attacks in the previous years had shown it also was easily overrun and burnt. Brick construction, popular in the Tidewater areas of the colonies where grand brick Georgian style mansions were rising, was simply too expensive in the western reaches of the colonies.

Fortunately, the Scotch-Irish and English had earlier brought to North America a structure that fit the bill perfectly. Additionally, Palatine settlers in the Mohawk River Valley of New York were already building these structures and closer to home, Jonathan Hager and several others had built fortified houses near to what is now Hagerstown, Maryland.

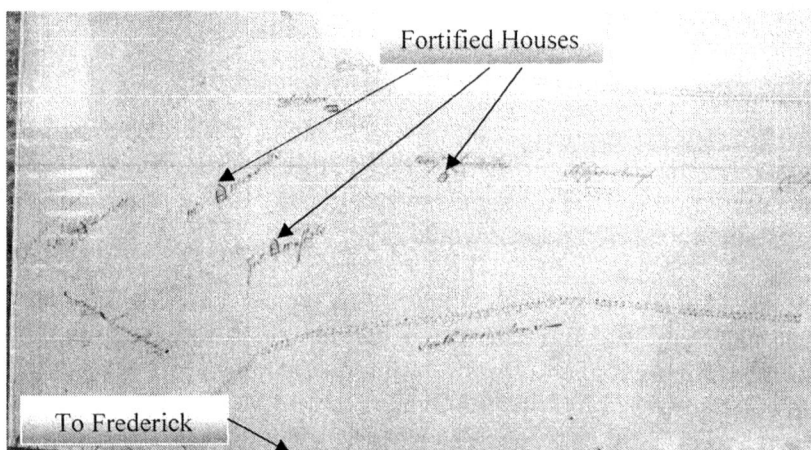

Reproduction of a 1756-57 map of fortifications in the Cumberland Valley, Courtesy of the American Philosophical Society
(Fortified Houses are the two story buildings with peaked roofs.)

Chapter V How The Fortified House Came To Fredericktown

A Short History of The Fortified House

The Fortified House is a unique architectural response devised by English and Scottish residents of sparsely settled border or coastal areas to protect themselves from hit-and-run attacks. Instead of living in walled medieval towns, as was the case in the Palatinate and most of Continental Europe, English, Scottish, and Irish rural populations were more scattered. Small crossroad settlements of a few houses or individual farmhouses were more the norm in the16[th] and17[th] Centuries.

During the dynastic and religious wars that ranged over the British Isles during that period, cavalry bands from the various factions harassed the population with hit-and-run attacks. Since there would not be time to escape to towns for defense, individual families started to fortify their homes. While we're most familiar with the royal castles or the large fortified manor houses of the gentry, the small landowner or tenant farmer needed protection as well.

In the most vulnerable regions, primarily the English-Scottish border and the southwestern coastal areas, English and Scottish yeoman built stone structures which are called "fortified houses" or "bastles" by current English historians. These were not grand structures. Often they were simple 20[ft.] x 30[ft.] field limestone buildings of one or two stories with large, well-built vaulted cellars, and slate roofs.

Bastle Routhly, Northumberland, 1723
Photo: English Heritage PastScape website

The purpose of a fortified house or a bastle (a bastle featured a first floor dedicated to housing animals) was completely defensive. No active defensive features such as outlying field works or additional garrisons for counter attacks were included. They were not designed or intended to ward off armies, only roving bands for several days.

These fortified houses and bastles, many from the 16th century, continued to be effective protection against numerous local threats and all-out wars in the 17th and 18th Centuries. These included the English Revolution in the middle of the 17th century, the English Civil War later in the 17th Century, various bands of English or Scottish "Border Reivers," and Barbary Pirates raiding Cornwall and Devon in southwest coastal England.

Many of these fortified houses along the Scottish-English border were also used as refuges by both sides in the 1745 "Bonnie Prince Charles" Jacobite uprising mentioned earlier.

Numerous examples of these fortified houses and bastles still remain in England and Scotland, mostly in the English-Scottish border region. For instance, a search of the English National Monument Record (about 400,000 records) contained on the English Heritage PastScape website for "bastle: 1550-1750" returned the following results for English border counties.

County	Number of Bastles: 1550-1750
Cumbria	105
Durham	7
Northumberland	199

In Scotland, numbers are equally as high, and interest in preserving them is higher. A fortified houses map is available, and the Scottish writer Nigel Tranter (1909-2000) published five volumes on the "Fortified Houses of Scotland" between 1962 and 1971. Granted, manor houses and castles are included as well, but five volumes is impressive.

The Fortified House and New York Palatine Settlements

While there are earlier examples of stone built fortified houses in New York (1676 in Kingston, NY) and Pennsylvania, those built in the Mohawk River Valley of New York have the greatest relevance to the Palatines in Fredericktown in 1756.

Palatines first arrived in great numbers in North America beginning around 1710. After nearly a century of continuous warfare in the Palatinate beginning with the Thirty Years War (1618-1648) many of the Protestant residents of the region were looking for peace or a new start. (Appendix III has a short history of the Palatinate emigration to North America.) England offered such an opportunity, indentured work in the New York Colony. Originally these immigrants, eventually numbering over 13,000, were brought to work on pine tar and turpentine plantations in the Hudson River Valley. Due to a number of poor management decisions, this enterprise failed.

The indentured Palatines were then moved west to plantations in the Mohawk Valley. After working off their terms of indenture, many were encouraged to settle west of the English settlements on cheap land to serve as a buffer between the English and the Iroquois Nation. This is quite similar to their settlement patterns in western Pennsylvania and Maryland.

To understand something about Palatines settlements in the Mohawk Valley at the time of the Seven Years War, we should start with William Johnson.

William Johnson

Perhaps the most important European colonial figure of the Mohawk Valley was William Johnson. He arrived in the 1730s from Ireland at the age of 23. In addition to managing his uncle's (British Vice Admiral Sir Peter Warren) property he began to assemble sizable land holdings of his own. He also started trading extensively with Native American tribes and eventually became the Colony of New York's chief tribal negotiator. Johnson gained a reputation among the Native tribes as a fair trader and reliable negotiator. He was made an honorary member of the Mohawk tribe of the Iroquois Nation. While he was held in high regard by the New York Royal Colonial government, he was somewhat mistrusted by the Pennsylvania and Virginia governments because of his support of Iroquois land claims in those colonies.

He also had relations with the Palatine settlers that seemed to go beyond the standard landlord-indentured relationship. He granted fur trading concessions along the Mohawk River to Palatinate families such as the Klocks, who will be discussed in more detail below. More important, his first wife, Katherine Wisenberg, was a Palatine indentured whose freedom he reputedly paid for. He had a son, John his heir, and two daughters with her.

Johnson and Braddock

In the original plans for the 1755 campaign that Braddock had drawn up, William Johnson was to have played an important role. Johnson had traveled to Alexandria, Virginia in April of 1755 to meet with Braddock and other colonial officials to plan the coming campaign. Among those participating in these meetings was Governor Horatio Sharpe of Maryland. In a letter to Johnson dated April 14, 1755, Braddock stated Johnson's objectives to include: 1) arranging for the support of the Iroquois Nation, and 2) preparing a force to rendezvous with Braddock at Ft. Niagara (Ft. Niagara, NY) to capture that French fort.

Johnson held a major conference with the Iroquois to discuss these plans. Approximately 600 Native tribal members attended the meeting in the summer of 1755 at his fortified house called Ft. Johnson.

Ft. Johnson, near Amsterdam, NY

The conference took place as Braddock was approaching Ft. Duquesne. Johnson was only able to secure the support of the Mohawk tribe of the Iroquois. However, the other five tribes agreed to remain neutral, at least for the time being. Once word of Braddock's defeat reached Johnson, the mission to Ft. Niagara was cancelled. The forces, both American militia and Mohawk, that Johnson had gathered instead marched north to Lake George to confront a French offensive led by the German mercenary Baron Dieskau. In September of 1755, forces led by Johnson defeated the French in a day-long bloody action known as the Battle of Lake George. Johnson was wounded in the early stages of the battle but recovered. As a result of this victory he was commissioned as the New York "Superintendent of all the affairs of the Six Nations and other Northern Indians" and made a baronet by King George II. He continued to play an important role in British-Indian negotiations as the war continued.

Katherine Wisenberg died in 1759. Sometime after that he began to live with Molly Brant, the sister of the Mohawk war Chief Joseph Brant, and had eight children with her. This union further cemented the ties between the Johnson family and the Mohawks. They would remain strong for over twenty more years.

William Johnson and Fortified Houses

Besides his other influences on life in the Mohawk Valley, William Johnson was instrumental in making the stone fortified house central to the defense of white settlers, especially the Palatinates that occupied the more western end of the valley.

Ft. Johnson (With Comparisons to Schifferstadt)

In 1746, he started construction of his limestone fort/trading station along the Mohawk River that was later called Ft. Johnson. Having come from the British Isles at a time when fortified houses were in active use along the English-Scottish border, and coming from a military family, Johnson would have been familiar with fortified house architecture and how to adapt it for his immediate use. Ft. Johnson is approximately 60$^{ft.}$ wide and 40$^{ft.}$ deep, or about twice the size of Schifferstadt. It has the expected two-foot thick stone walls that while providing protection from most weapons of the time made the house nearly impossible to keep warm in winter. But, such were the tradeoffs that had to be made on the frontier.

At the time, it was probably the largest house this far west in New York. Like Schifferstadt it has two main floors, a cellar, and a very tall attic. At Ft. Johnson the attic is tall enough to be divided into two levels. Also like Schifferstadt, it was not located on a spring (there were no springs on either property) which some consider a primary characteristic of a fortified house. Instead residents of both buildings relied on wells for drinking water. Water for other uses at both buildings was provided by streams that ran about the same distance from each building.

During times of pending attacks, enough drinking water for several days would have been collected from the springs and stored in casks in the cellars of these buildings.

Ft. Johnson from Hall Creek

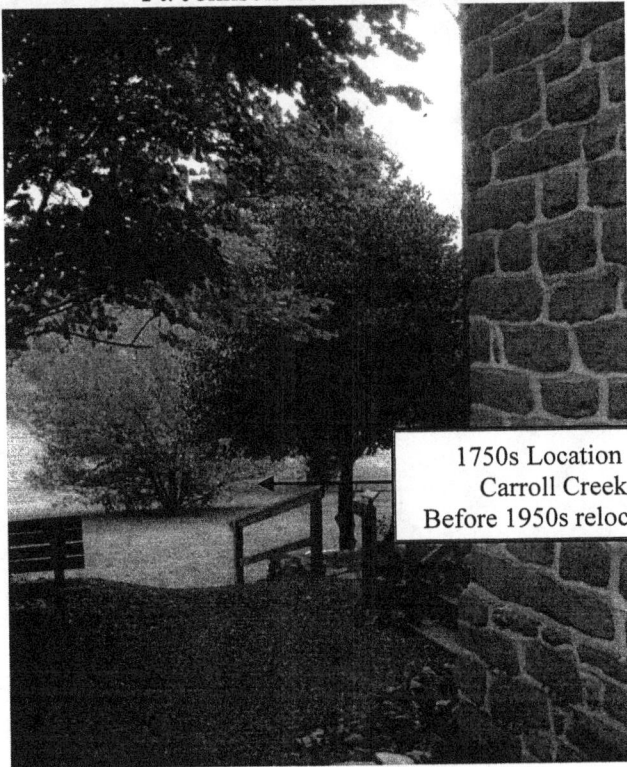

1750s Location of
Carroll Creek
Before 1950s relocation

Schifferstadt Looking South

Ft. Johnson was first finished in 1749. Additional buildings, including a barn and a mill were added prior to 1755. After 1755, a stockade that connected the main house and outbuildings was added for extra protection as shown in this 1759 drawing by Johnson's son-in-law Guy Johnson.

Key to Guy Johnson's 1759 Sketch of Fort Johnson

A - The House B - The wall and ramparts C - Corner block-house D - The Cooper's House
E - The Bake house F - Pigeon house G - The Mill H - aqueduct
I - Indian Council House K - Indian encampments L - Sheep House M - Large barn
N - Mount Johnson O - Johnson's old house P - old barn Q - The Mohawk River
R - Island S - 13 smaller islands T - Block House - for defense for back of house
V - Creek W - Garden X - Pastures Y - Cornfields Z - Road to Schenectady

Ft. Johnson during the Seven Year War
A Sketch by Guy Johnson, William Johnson'sSon-in-Law

Looking closely at this 1759 sketch also reveals that the back side of the building, the side most vulnerable to attack, did not have a door during the Seven Years War. Also it had only two windows. After the war, when the building was occupied by his son John Johnson and his wife, a door and another window was added.

Detail of 1759 Guy Johnson Sketch (north wall)

North wall with later modifications

Interestingly enough, during the 1970s architectural survey of Schifferstadt, evidence showed that the door and at least one window on the back of the house, the vulnerable west facing side, were added some time after its initial construction in the 1750s.

Back (west) wall of Schifferstadt

Mohawk Valley Palatinate Fortified Houses and Schifferstadt

Besides building Ft. Johnson, William Johnson also encouraged the building of fortified houses throughout the Mohawk Valley. By 1756, approximately twenty-five fortified houses had been built. Many of them had been built by and were occupied by Palatine families. These included Fort Frey, Ft. Herkimer, five at German Flatts, and Ft. Klock (1750).

Fort Klock, 1750
St. Johnsville, New York

Ft. Klock is located about twenty miles west of Ft. Johnson. It is close to the Mohawk River and was built as a fur trading station by members of the Klock family that had emigrated from the Palatinate sometime around 1720 to work on the pine-tar plantations. Since William Johnson supervised the fur trade along the Mohawk, he probably was closely involved in setting up this station and probably provided advice on construction and the selection of stone masons as well.

Fort Klock is a good example of the typical Mohawk Valley Palatinate fortified house. The 1750 building has two stories, a cellar, and an attic. It is about $20^{ft.}$ by $40^{ft.}$ and was probably built by traveling professional stone masons. Note the quality of the 1750 details compared to the 1764 addition that was built by the Klock family.

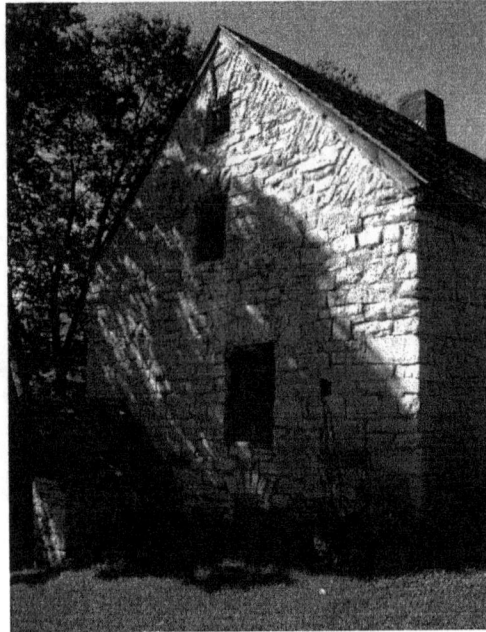

Original 1750 Fort
Note "Eyebrow" Treatment over Windows, Keystone at Roof Peak,
& Uniform Stone Size

1764 Addition
Note Simplified Window Lintels, no Keystone &
Non-Uniform Stone Size

Ft. Klock does have a spring in the cellar. However, in order to locate the fort over the spring, the Klock's had to put the building in a weak defensive position - at the foot of a hill rising to the north away from the river. This less than ideal position allowed attackers to take level shots at the second floor while defenders on the first floor would have to make more difficult uphill shots. (In a later 1780 battle during the Revolutionary War, a woman on the second floor was wounded by a musket ball shot through a second floor loophole.) The lesson seems to be that there are always tradeoffs when it comes to selecting a location to build a fortified house.

Ft. Klock: Looking Down From the North

Connections Between Mohawk Palatine Fortified Houses and Schifferstadt

In addition to the previously noted similarities between Fort Johnson and Schifferstadt, there are five structural similarities that Mohawk Valley Palatine fortified houses (as exemplified by Ft. Klock) and Palatinate Schifferstadt share. These are: 1) German or Dutch center fireplaces (instead of being located on outside walls), 2) "eyebrow" stonework over windows, 3) "splayed" interior windows, 4) the location and structure of the stairs from the cellar, and 5) "Palatine Pink" interior paint.

Ft. Klock   Schifferstadt

German/Dutch Center Fireplaces

"Eyebrow" Window Treatment

"Splayed" Interior Window Treatment

Location of Cellar Staircase

In both Ft. Klock and Schifferstadt the staircase from the cellar enters directly into the floor of the kitchen. This is different than the method we're most familiar with of stairs coming up to a door that can be closed to regulate the temperature on each floor. In order to provide a similar type of barrier, wooden walls had to be built around the stairwell opening. Both Ft. Klock and Schifferstadt show similar evidence of where the stairs came up and where walls were built.

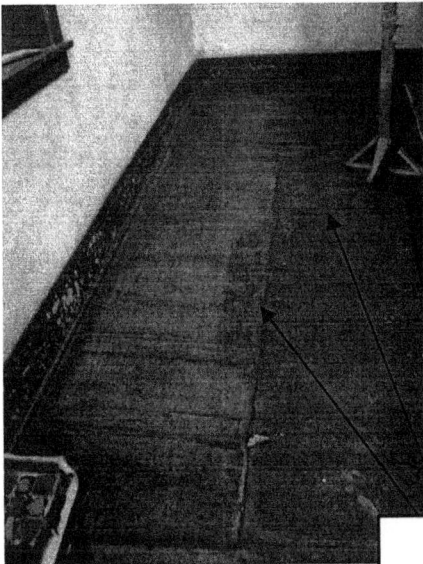

Ft. Klock   **Schifferstadt**

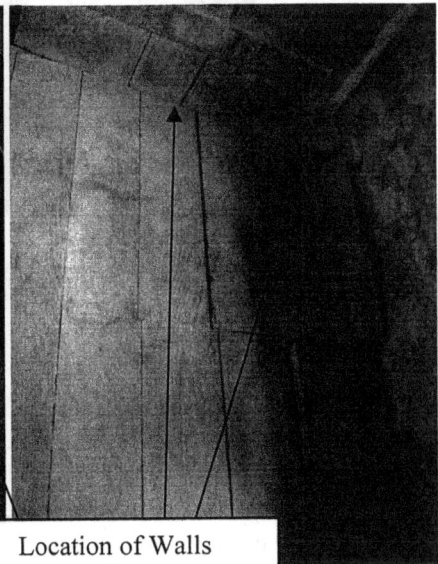

Location of Walls
&
Stairwells

Palatine Pink Paint

When walls were scraped during renovations at Ft Johnson, Ft. Klock, and Schifferstadt, as well as other buildings of the period in the Mohawk Valley, they all revealed numerous patches of a pinkish-red paint throughout the buildings. These patches are all visible when on tours of these sites. (Unfortunately, this edition of the book does not have color photos so these patches are not included.) This color is referred to as "Palatine Pink" in the Mohawk Valley.

Loop Holes

There is one other feature of fortified houses that Schifferstadt should share with the Mohawk Valley fortified houses – loop holes. These are holes, at the height of a shouldered musket, placed in the stone walls to allow defenders inside to fire muskets or rifles at attackers.

Since these buildings were constructed in the 1740s and 1750s there have been many changes made to them. As mentioned earlier, occupants added doors and windows. Loop holes were also changed. Except in building restorations that specifically include the loopholes as part of the interpretive history, they are now usually filled in. In most cases, occupants of the houses filled in the loopholes some time after the danger periods had passed to keep out cold air. (Even during the periods of danger, stones, pieces of wood, or rags were used to stuff the loopholes to keep out the cold.)

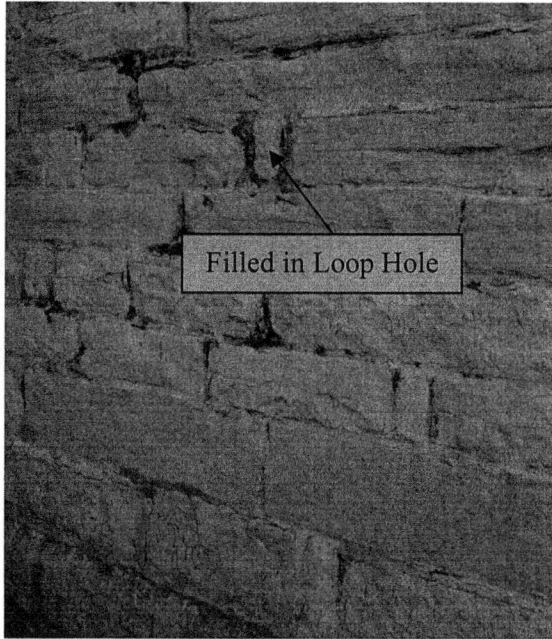

Ft. Herkimer Church/Fort
German Flatts, New York

In many of the restored fortified houses of the Mohawk Valley the loop holes were either restored to, or left in their Seven Years War configuration. At Schifferstadt this is not the case. In the 1970s the exterior was restored. At the time there was no search for loopholes and the amount of mortar used for re-pointing was so excessive that the current appearance of the wall is not what it would have been in the late 1750s. However, in looking closely at the exterior walls at Schifferstadt, along a line that would be at the level of a shouldered musket, there are several very interesting stone and mortar formations that look like they could have been loopholes. The following photos compare loop holes from the Mohawk Valley to possible loop holes at Schifferstadt. They are all to the approximately same scale for comparison purposes.

In the first set of photos it looks like one or possibly two stones were placed in the loop hole at Schifferstadt and extra mortar added during the 1970 work. (These probably were considered "loose stones" during the renovation.) Notice also the irregular shape of stones around the loop hole at Ft. Klock The second and third set of photos seems to show the best comparison in terms of size and shape.

Mohawk Valley   **Schifferstadt**

Ft. Klock

Herkimer Church

Ft. Klock

These are not necessarily positive identifications and additional research on the interior construction of the walls would have to be done. However, the position and number of these locations are consistent with the loopholes found in other fortified houses in the Mohawk Valley.

From The Mohawk Valley to Fredericktown

When all these physical comparisons are taken together with the continuous communications we know took place between the Palatine communities, it seems very reasonable to conclude that the Brunners of Fredericktown had knowledge of the fortified houses in the Mohawk Valley.

Also, with their work on fortified houses in the Mohawk Valley largely completed by 1756, itinerant stone masons might have made the trip south to Fredericktown and its environs looking for work. In light of this information, Schifferstadt seems to be a William Johnson inspired, Palatinate constructed Mohawk Valley style fortified house.

Attacks at German Flatts, New York

As mentioned earlier, Palatine settlers did build five fortified houses (destroyed during the construction of the Erie Canal) in a settlement near Ft. Herkimer called German Flatts. Unfortunately, they initially threw away the safety that these buildings offered. They failed to heed warnings in November of 1757 given by Mohawk scouts serving with British and American forces that an attack was coming. They did not take refuge in the fortified houses and consequently suffered greatly. Many of the inhabitants were killed or scalped and about 150 were taken captive. The attack was led by a French officer, M. de Belestre, who had been captured near Ft. Cumberland, Maryland in June of 1757. (He most likely escaped; prisoners were generally not released during this war.)

There was also an attack on the settlement the next year, 1758. This time the Palatine settlers took cover in the fortified houses during that battle. The attack was easily repulsed by militia that had been gathered at Ft. Herkimer, about a mile away, and the settlers did not suffer any casualties.

German Flatts looking east toward Ft. Herkimer
The Erie Canal is behind the tree-line

Herkimer Church converted to a fort

Chapter VI Schifferstadt In Time of War

By the autumn of 1756, people in Fredericktown, both residents and refugees must have started to feel isolated, especially those of German-speaking descent. The Indian and French campaign, not only blocked the way west but essentially cut off the roads north and south as well. This must have had a major economic and social effect on the town, especially the cutting of the northern road. Since most of the Palatine residents of western Maryland had first landed in Philadelphia, many of them first settled in the German-speaking communities of Lancaster County before heading west. Many ties had been established with those communities. As a result, the wagon road (US 15) from Fredericktown to Harris's Landing (Harrisburg, Pa) and on to Lancaster County was, in times of peace, heavily traveled. In addition, the road north from Harrisburg (now US 11 or US 15) also led directly to the Palatine settlements in the Mohawk Valley. Agricultural products were traded. Furniture and iron products made in Lancaster County were brought south to Frederick County. Ministers moved from town to town, and spouses came from families that belonged to the same religious movement. This "German Highway" was the main artery of the German-speaking community in the American colonies. Cutting it must have further heightened the alarm first brought on by the rush of refugees. During this time, the recently arrived minister at the German Reformed Church in Fredericktown wrote a letter to his superiors in Philadelphia complaining about being stuck in Fredericktown and asking for relief, which did not come.

Now, the only safe way to Lancaster County was the roundabout route of first going east to Baltimore and then north along the Chesapeake Bay to the Delaware colony and then northwest back into Pennsylvania.

Life at Schifferstadt

While the exterior and general layout of the building is a British/Scottish inspired fortified house, the first floor retained the traditional Palatinate layout. It has a four-room arrangement with center hall (Durchgängigen Haus), and a central chimney separating the kitchen from the living area. It was also typical in the Palatinate tradition to access the second floor by a steep winding stair to one side of the center hall to save space.

The second floor was divided into two great rooms on either side of the central hall. (The 2nd floor at Ft. Klock was also divided into two rooms by the central fireplace.) During this period, these rooms were probably used as dormitories segregated by gender. Each was heated by some type of fireplace. Later, "jamb" or five-plate stoves were installed that were fed wood from the central hallway. One, dated 1758, and produced in Pennsylvania, is still in its original location.

2nd Floor 5-Plate Stove

The attic of Schifferstadt has as high a ceiling as the other floors of the house. Besides being a food storage space, extra bedding and possessions of frontier refugees were probably stored there as well.

Attic at Schifferstadt

While it is impossible to know exactly how life went on at Schifferstadt when attacks seemed imminent, a general idea of living conditions can be drawn.

Most likely, the immediate family of Elias Brunner, who is listed as the owner of the property, as well as Joseph Brunner, his father, lived on the first floor. Since there is no evidence of similar fortified houses on the other Brunner properties, the families of Henry, John, and Jacob Brunner most likely lived in log or wooden houses and spent much of the time in their individual dwellings. However, when alarms were given, news of nearby attacks arrived, or when conditions just seemed uncertain, some or all of these three families probably took overnight refuge at Schifferstadt. Being family members, some of them probably stayed on the first floor as space allowed. Other Brunner adults probably occupied the 2nd floor rooms while the boys and girls found space where they could.

The 2nd floor rooms also probably had more permanent occupants, Reformed Church members or Palatinate kinsmen whom had been driven out of the Cumberland Valley. And, although unheated, the attic was probably used by children and others when space ran out downstairs.

Schifferstadt was most likely crowded and often punctuated by the cries of the newborn. Probably one or more of the births recorded by the German Reformed Church took place there. Farm work, cloth making from flax or wool, and food preservation dominated when weather and daylight allowed. And with the extra manpower available, as well as extra mouths to feed, the four Brunner properties were most likely farmed to the maximum. Trees cleared to make way for fields were chopped for firewood to be used in the main and 2nd floor fireplaces or stoves.

One would probably have seen the first floor fireplace lit all day for cooking. Women probably took turns preparing boiled and roasted meats, various baked goods, and cooked vegetables. Young boys and girls were probably enlisted to bring in firewood and water from the well just west of the building, or from nearby Carroll Creek. In addition, adequate emergency water and food supplies for at least two or three days had to be maintained in the cellar. Nighttime brought bible readings and prayer as they all hoped their God and the 24-inch thick fieldstone walls would deliver them to a time of peace.

Recreation of the Palatinate Village Culture

In some ways, this forced creation of a community allowed the residents of Schifferstadt to recreate the village culture they had in the Palatinate without interference from the dominant English culture. A patriarchal kinship based social system could be re-established with Joseph Brunner the leader once again of "klein Schifferstadt". The pressure to "anglicize" or to speak or write the English language would have been removed as well. What was happening at Schifferstadt was probably happening at other Palatine residences throughout Pennsylvania and Maryland where refugees from the Cumberland Valley and other western areas were staying. This re-establishment of their culture probably contributed in large part to the ability of this community to maintain a separate identity throughout the 18th, 19th and 20th Centuries while other communities quickly assimilated.

There is, however, one question about these times that stands out: were there many firearms at Schifferstadt? Besides the expected hunting pieces, was there a cache of muskets or rifles available? The possibility of loop holes argues for this. Were armed guards stationed on the western ends of the fields as crops were planted or harvested? Was a watch kept at night? Hopefully the answers to how they balanced their religious beliefs with the security realities will one day be discovered in accounts found in somebody's attic.

Hanging On: 1757

While the news arriving through August of 1756 had been uniformly bleak, by mid September news of an unbelievable victory began arriving in places like Fredericktown. On September 8th a Pennsylvania Scotch-Irish militia force led by John Armstrong, a hard-bitten veteran of the unsuccessful Scottish Jacobite rebellion in 1745, attacked and destroyed the "command-and-control center" of Kittanning. Armstrong had obtained detailed information about Kittanning, probably from prisoners that had escaped or been released, and put together a well-planned raid. He timed the raid in phase with the moon so that his force of about 300 men would have sufficient light for night marches and used moonset and sunrise data to time the attack.

His raiding party traveled west over the same trails used by the French and Indian war-parties. By traveling at night and being extremely careful, they remained undetected for the entire length of the over one hundred mile journey. They achieved complete surprise when they attacked just before sunrise and succeeded in burning most of the village, blowing up most of the gunpowder that had been cached, and destroying many of the stored weapons. They also killed the Lenape war chief known as Captain Jacobs. Unfortunately, most of the settlers that had been held there were not found. Only a few were released. The Pennsylvania Gazette of September 23, 1756 carried a very detailed report of the raid based on Armstrong's post-battle account. Some of the details of that account are as follows.

"And the Indians generally refusing Quarters, when was offered them, declaring they were Men, and would not be prisoners."

"Col. Armstrong (who now received a wound in his shoulder by a Musket Ball) ordered their Houses to be set on fire over their heads, which was immediately done by the Officers and Soldiers with great Activity."

"it was computed that in all between 30& 40" were destroyed, tho' we bro't off but 12 Scalps."

"Eleven English Prisoners were released."

"In the whole we had killed 17 wounded 13 missing nine."

An enlarged photocopy of Col. Armstrong's plan for the Kittanning Raid
Displayed at the Conococheague Institute in July 2007,
Courtesy of the American Philosophical Society

In the immediate aftermath of the raid, Kittanning was abandoned by the
Lenape and Shawanoe. But, the raid did not stop attacks in the
Cumberland Valley. On November 1st the fort at Mc Dowell's Mill was
attacked and destroyed. Colonel Armstrong responded by building a new
stockaded fort several miles north called Fort Loudon. It was finished in
December, 1756.

Indian and French raids in Maryland and Pennsylvania did decrease in 1757. While the destruction of Kittanning probably contributed to this decrease three other factors were at play as well.

First, after the success of the raids in 1756, there simply weren't that many targets left. Most of the farms had been destroyed and most of the people had been driven out. The few people remaining were clustered in fortified or stockaded houses.

Second, by the spring of 1757 Virginia began sending Cherokee warriors to Ft. Cumberland and the still incomplete Ft. Frederick to patrol. On April 28, 1757: The Pennsylvania Gazette published a letter from "A Gentleman from Conococheague" who reported favorably on the quality of the Catawba warriors that were garrisoning Ft. Cumberland, *are chiefly old Experienced Warriors and among them eight War Captains who seem all hearty in the English Interest."*

Its also reported in the Maryland Gazette in April that Cherokee Indians arrived at Ft. Frederick thinking at first they are still in Virginia. *"but coming to this Fort, found we were in another Province."* And, discovering they are in Maryland, asked Governor Sharpe for provisions,

> *"I hope our Good Brother [Governor Sharpe] will not be backward in providing Necessaries for us. I have sent you a List of what is useful to us,"*

The Gazette reported that Sharpe did not provide the necessary supplies but instead offered the Cherokee Indians at Ft. Frederick rewards for killing or scalping the French and their Indian allies,

> *"I will give you a Present as large as that which I have now sent you, for every two Enemies that you shall take Prisoners, and deliver upon to me, or that you shall kill, and bring me the Scalps of, or I will give you the Value thereof in Money."*

On May 19, 1757 The Maryland Gazette reported that the Cherokees intercepted and broke up a raiding party near Rays Town (present-day Bedford, Pa).

> *"The Scalps and Prisoners are brought to Fort Frederick, where the Cherokees will remain till they here from the Governor and receive their reward."*

Third, because of the success in 1756, the French command in Quebec moved troops and supplies destined for Ft. Duquesne to the Lake Champlain region of New York where they would be used in a major campaign to drive the English south. The primary French success of that campaign was the capture of Fort William Henry at the south end of Lake George. The fort, commanded by Col. George Munro, was forced to surrender on August 9, 1757 to Marquis de Montcalm when Gen. Daniel Webb, the new commander of the 48th regiment that camped in Frederick two years earlier, refused to march to their aid from Ft. Edward which was about 12 miles away.

When the British marched out of the fort under a flag of truce, British soldiers, American militia, camp followers, and wounded left in a hospital, were massacred by Indians allied with the French. Outrage built throughout the colonies when accounts of the massacre become known. The outrage further increased when survivors accused Montcalm of doing nothing to stop the massacre of those who had been promised safe passage. If you have ever seen the 1992 movie *"Last of the Mohicans,"* this is the battle that is depicted.

This is not to say that all attacks near Fredericktown stopped in 1757. In June and July a cluster of attacks were reported which indicates that one or more war-parties had been dispatched from Ft. Duquesne, which had taken over the function of Kittanning. Among these attacks was an ambush of a patrol from Ft. Loudon that resulted in fifteen of the twenty-five men being killed. For the people in Fredericktown, probably the scariest attack occurred on July 27th. Alexander M'Keasy who lived on Tom's Creek, about fifteen miles northeast of Fredericktown was killed, his son was captured, and a slave girl wounded. This raid was the first one recorded east of South and Catoctin Mountains. This meant that the residents and refugees of Fredericktown and the Catoctin Valley were now as vulnerable as their kinsmen who lived in the Cumberland Valley or further west.

Meanwhile, the conflict between the Maryland Assembly and Governor Sharpe over Ft. Frederick continued. Construction continued, albeit slowly, but still Maryland did not provide any money for garrisoning it or Ft. Cumberland.

Any immediate protection would have to be provided from Washington's Virginia forces and Pennsylvania militia.

As the winter of 1757-58 approached, the people in Fredericktown must have wondered if this war was ever going to end. What would 1758 bring? Death and destruction or deliverance?

Reconstructed Wall at Ft. Frederick
Note that the original portion of the wall is about 2/3 the height of the
reconstructed wall

Chapter VII 1758

Since William Pitt was appointed leader (the term Prime Minister was not yet used) of the English government in December 1756, he had been trying to find the resources to launch offensive operations in North America. Unfortunately, most of these plans had to wait until he had acquired enough backing in Parliament, reformed the fiscal operation of the King's government, rebuilt relations with the colonies, and replaced most of the senior military commanders. The year 1758 would see the first fruits of his labors. In April, General John Forbes arrived in Philadelphia to take command of an expedition that was planned to capture Ft. Duquesne and bring the Indian tribes allied with the French into the British sphere of influence.

Besides the arrival of Forbes and more British regulars, other conditions were beginning to change.

Throughout late 1757 and early 1758, reports of Ohio Indian dissatisfaction with the French began to trickle in. Thinking there might be an opening, the "Peace Quaker" faction in Pennsylvania, led by Israel Pemberton and the Friendly Association began pushing for peace talks. Throughout the spring and summer, Pemberton, Forbes, William Johnson, Iroquois leaders, and eastern Lenape chiefs exchanged messages and wampum belts. The extraordinary shrewdness and sophistication of the Iroquois's tactics during this period would put the statescraft of later European diplomats such as Tallyrand or Churchill to shame.

The full story of these negotiations deserves a much more detailed treatment. Fortunately it exists in Francis Jennings, *Empire of Fortune.* Jennings does an admirable job of not only explaining the diplomacy of the Seven Years War in North America, but also of elucidating its historical importance.

Meanwhile, while the diplomacy was progressing, Forbes's health was nearly destroyed by his efforts to build and supply an army at Carlisle. At first Pennsylvania did not provide supplies, but later relented and provided all the supplies necessary. The Carolinas and the New England colonies refused to provide troops or supplies because they had expeditions they considered more important to their own interests. Closer to his base at Carlisle, Maryland once more refused to provide troops, supplies, or money to pay for the expedition. Only Pennsylvania and Virginia provided troops and support for the expedition. Washington arrived with a force of 1,000 and Pennsylvania provided another 2,700.

This final overwhelming lack of support from Maryland at such a crucial juncture would have both short and long term negative consequences for the colony. To begin with, when Washington proposed to Forbes that the expedition should follow Braddock's 1755 route through Maryland and Virginia the idea was completely rejected. While some historians treat this rejection as a result of a personal battle between Forbes and Washington, it seems reasonable that the lack of support by the people of Fredericktown in 1755 and the lack of support by Maryland in 1758 played an important part as well. Simply put, why would Forbes want to take his much larger force of about 7,000 through a region that did not support the forces Dunbar brought through that were about 1/10 in number?

In the longer term, the colony that would have the military road that was used to capture Ft. Duquesne would benefit economically since that road would be considered the safest route west. Land prices would soar along the successful road as stage stops, inns, taverns, and later towns were built.

Forbes selected a route through Pennsylvania. From Carlisle the route would first run from Ft. Loudon to Ft. Littleton and then to Raystown (Bedford, Pa). From there a new road running directly to Ft. Duquesne would be cut. This route also had the advantage of not having to cross either the Monongahela or Allegheny Rivers. (Present day US 30 follows much of Forbes Road.)

Forbes took his time moving west. This was for two reasons. First, Forbes wanted to make sure that his army would be adequately supplied. He did this by advancing in stages rather than making a headlong rush like Braddock did from Jumonville to Ft. Duquesne. As Forbes reached each fort, he waited to advance until all the supplies were brought up. Then he would advance to the next fort.

The second reason he was not in a hurry was because of the progress of the negotiations with the Indian tribes. It seemed if he waited long enough, the French would lose their Indian allies and Ft. Duquesne might be captured without much of a fight.

Forbes' army had reached Loyalhanna (present day Ligonier, Pa) about forty or so miles from Ft. Duquesne by September. Rains had slowed the advance but also the potential for a breakthrough was in the making back in eastern Pennsylvania.

The colonies of Pennsylvania and New Jersey were jointly sponsoring the Easton Treaty Conference that started on October 8th. It would continue until the 26th. With Israel Pemberton pressing all parties toward peace, there were major results. By the closing of the conference, the Iroquois and the eastern and western Lenape were back in the English fold. In addition, some of the "Ohio tribes" including some Shawanoe groups backed away from the French. In return, the British made substantial promises to the Native tribes.

Three primary promises were made.

> First, western Pennsylvania and New York treaty lands were returned to the Iroquois Confederation and the western Lenape.

> Second, lands in the Ohio Valley were granted to the Ohio tribes. (There was more Iroquois involvement with these lands than the Ohio tribes wanted, but that problem was put off to a later date.)

> Third, and probably the hardest promise to deliver on, Pennsylvania, New York, Delaware, and the Crown government guaranteed that white settlers would be prevented from settling the Ohio Valley. In addition, the Covenant Chain was temporarily re-established.

As outlandish as these promises sound, the various tribes agreed and warriors stopping the advance of Forbes began to slip away and return to their villages in the Ohio country. From the distance of 250 years, it seems that the tribes made the jump from the French to the English for a very simple reason: The English were growing in strength and aligning with them offered the best chance of retaining their territory.

After several skirmishes in September and October, all actually won tactically by the French and the remaining Indians, on the night of November 24, 1758, the French abandoned and burnt Ft. Duquesne. The British occupied the burned out hulk of the fort the next day.

Colonel Bouquet, the English second in command, attributed the success of the campaign to General Forbes.

> *"After God the success of this Expedition is intirely due to the General, who by bringing about the Treaty of Easton, had struck the blow which has knocked the French in the head, in temporizing wisely to expect the Effects of the Treaty, in securing all his posts, and giving nothing to chance, and not yielding to the urging instances for taking Braddock's Road, which could have been our destruction.''*

Washington felt it was a result of the weakness of the French and Indians.

> *"the possession of this fort has been matter of great surprise to the whole army, and we cannot attribute it to more probable causes than those of weakness, want of provisions, and desertion of their Indians."*

Peace Comes to Fredericktown

The fall of Ft. Duquesne and the effects of the Treaty of Easton virtually stopped the raids in New York, Pennsylvania, Maryland and Virginia. By the spring of 1759 those Palatinate kinsmen from the Cumberland Valley that had spent all or part of the past two years in Fredericktown began to return to their destroyed homes and farms. The graph of Fredericktown christening shows this with a decrease in the number of christenings at the Reform Church to thirty-four in 1759 and to twenty in 1760. Even the later rapid growth of Fredericktown did not increase christenings to the level of 1757-58.

Seven Years War Fredericktown Christenings
German Reformed and All Saints Churches

Christenings/Year

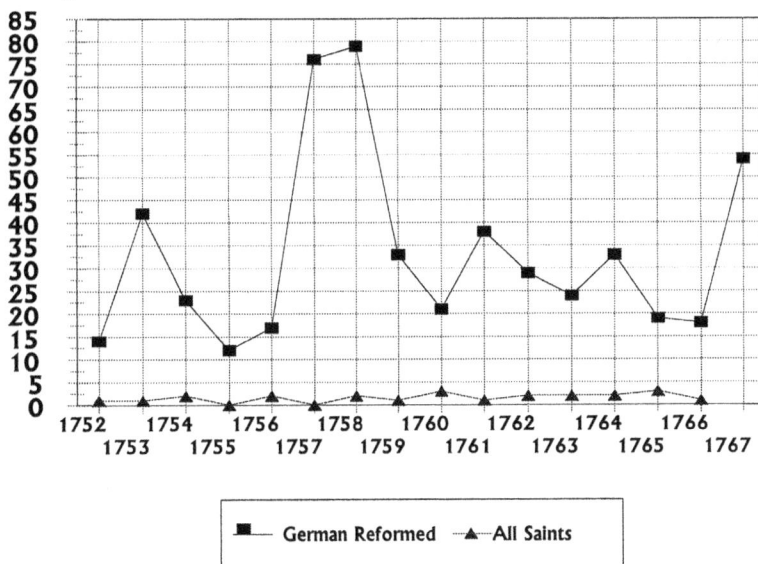

Legend: ■— German Reformed ▲—All Saints

By 1760, thoughts of needing forts or fortified houses were probably receding from the minds of most people in Frederick County. From the historical record, it appears they were more concerned with getting England (rather than Maryland) to pay for the late war so they could concentrate on becoming more prosperous.

The Seven Year's War continued until 1763. Quebec fell in the winter of 1759 after a particularly bloody battle on the Plains of Abraham where both the French commander Montcalm and the English commander Wolfe were killed. French Canada formally surrendered in September 1760. The war continued on the European continent and in places such as India and the Philippines. In early 1763 the Treaty of Paris that formally ended the war was signed. The Treaty included something called the "Proclamation Line." According to the treaty, American settlers were restricted to lands east of the Proclamation Line. This was a northeast-southwest line corresponding to the most western of the Appalachian ridges. The Proclamation Line enforced the promise made in the Treaty of Easton. In addition, terms of the treaty allowed British troops to occupy all French forts in the Ohio River Valley and Great Lakes basin.

71

Postscript: Pontiac's War

By mid 1763 all the tribes that had been party to the Treaty of Easton, as well all the remaining tribes of the Ohio, had clear indications that the promises made in the treaty were empty. White settlers were pouring into western treaty lands and crossing into the Ohio country in total disregard of the Proclamation Line. Furthermore, the tribes felt the British occupation of the French forts was a violation of the Treaty of Easton.

In western Ohio a charismatic Ottawa war chief by the name of Pontiac had a vision that the whites, all whites, must be removed from the continent. This vision became a religious mission for the tribes of the Ohio country. It was soon translated into action. Their attacks combined a fury not seen in the Seven Years War with the impressive tactics they had developed in that late war. The Iroquois United Nations joined in and for the first time since Europeans first stepped ashore in North America all the eastern tribes were fighting on the same side. All settlements west of the Ohio were destroyed and virtually all in the western lands of Virginia, Maryland, Pennsylvania, and New York. Again long trains of refugees arrived in Fredericktown, Carlisle, and Winchester, cities of refuge just five years earlier.

The Maryland Gazette published the following report from Fredericktown on July 19, 1763.

> *"Every day, for some time past, has offered the melancholy scene of poor distressed families driving downwards through this town with their effects, who have deserted their plantations for fear of falling into the cruel hands of our savage enemies, now daily seen in the woods. And never was panic more general or forcible than that of the back inhabitants, whose terrors at this time exceed what followed on the defeat of Gen. Braddock, when the frontiers lay open to the incursions of both French and Indians."*

At least the importance of Conococheague was now recognized.

> *"Whilst Conococheague settlement stands firm we shall think ourselves in some sort of security from the insults here. But should the inhabitants there give way, you should see your city and the lower counties crowded*

with objects of compassion, as flight would in case become general."

With continued attacks in the Cumberland Valley more people evacuated to Fredericktown. It's probably safe to assume that Schifferstadt was once more opened to kinsmen having to once more flee their farms. (Christening at the Reformed Church increased from 25 in 1763 to 34 in 1764 and decreased to 19 in 1765.)

Pontiac's War became particularly nasty, even by the standards of the time. Ft. Pitt was cutoff and surrounded. The British troops at the fort utilized biological warfare to try to raise the siege. Infected blankets were purposely distributed by British troops to cause a smallpox epidemic. The Ft. Pitt account book reports that on June 24, 1763 two blankets and two handkerchiefs were presented to two Delaware chiefs.

"To sundries got to Replace in kind those which were taken from people in the Hospital to Convey the Small-pox to the Indians,"

Disease did weaken the Indian forces as Bouquet approached to raise the siege. Indians attacked his force at Bushy Run (east of Pittsburgh), but were defeated when Bouquet counter-ambushed the attacking Indians. It seemed that Bouquet had learned how to conduct "Indian style" warfare and had trained his troops well.

The winter of 1763-64 was reminiscent of the winter of 1756-57 in many colonial towns including Fredericktown. Western settlers were seeking refuge and everyone was wondering if the spring would bring more destruction or peace?

In the spring of 1764 Bouquet brought the war to an end with a scorched-earth expedition into the Ohio country. Major Ottawa, Mingo, Shawanoe, and other tribal villages were destroyed. Crops were burned and men, women, and children were scalped and killed. For the time being an uneasy peace was restored. An estimated 2,000 people were killed in the approximate nine months of the war.

Refugees again started back to their farms and houses in the summer of 1764. The people of Fredericktown breathed a sigh of relief. They had again provided Shelter from the Storm. Would they ever have to provide it again?

Source Material

Forward

1. The statement about sea battles in the Seven Years War is based on information in:

   Mahan, A.T., The Influence of Sea Power on History, Williamstown, MA: Corner House Publishers, 1978.

Introduction

1. The quote from the British officer is from the diary of a naval officer with the artillery detachment. Some writers think this may be Lieutenant Charles Spendelow. This version of the quote is from:

   Wahll, Andrew J., Braddock Road Chronicles 1755, Westminster, MD: Heritage Books, 1999.

Chapter I Peace and War 1748-1754

1. Information on the emigration of the Brunners and their land ownership is from:

   Osborn, David Lewis, Joseph Brunner of Rothenstein, Schifferstadt and Frederick, Lee's Summit, Missouri: Published by the author. 1991, pp. 17-20.

   Forbes, Meg, "The Brunner Family of Frederick, Maryland: A study of the early German settlers in Frederick," Frederick, Maryland: Hood College, unpublished manuscript, 1978

2. The statement on the relations between the Frederick County Sherriff and the Palatinate immigrants is based on research presented in:

   Rice, James Douglas, Crime and punishment in Frederick County and Maryland, 1748-1837: A study in culture, society, and law, Ann Arbor, Michigan: UMI, 1994.

3. Information on Palatine settlements in the Cumberland Valley is from:

   Stauffer, John, "German Immigrants on the Harle, 1736," unpublished, vertical file, Conococheague Institute, Mercersburg, PA.

4. The map of Brunner land ownership is based on the map on page 259 in:

   Dern, John P. & Grace L.Tracey, <u>Pioneers of Old Monocacy, The Early Settlement of Frederick County, Maryland 1721-1743</u>, Baltimore, Maryland: Genealogical Publishing Co., 1989. Hereafter cited as Dern & Tracy.

5. The Interprovincial Congress is discussed in Chapter Five, "The Last Congress at Albany" of:

   Jennings, Francis, <u>Empire of Fortune</u>, New York: W.W. Norton, 1988, pp. 95-101.

6. Thanks to Dr. Walter Powell for providing key clarifications on events at Jumonville Glen and Ft. Necessity.

Chapter II The Braddock Defeat: 1755

1. The Daniel Dulany Jr. quotes are from:

   Older, Curtis, <u>The Braddock Expedition and Fox's Gap in Maryland</u>, Westminster, MD: Family Lines Publishers, 1995, p. 34

2. Information on the defeat of Varius in AD 9 is from:

   Schama, Simon, <u>Landscape and Memory</u>, New York: Vintage Books, 1995.

3. Thanks to Dr. Walter Powell for providing key clarifications on events at the Battle of Monongahela.

4. The number of cannons lost in the battle are from:

   "Return of Ordnance by Thomas Ord and James Furnis, 18 July 1755" as published in <u>Military Affairs in North America 1748-1765</u>, edited by Stanley Pargellis, Hamden, CT: Archon Books, 1969, pp. 96-97

5. Quotes from Charlotte Browne are from her unpublished diary, 1754-56, located at the US Library of Congress Manuscript Room, Washington DC.

Chapter III Total War on the Frontier

1. Information on the campaign relies primarily on information produced by the Conococheague Institute in Mercersburg, Pennsylvania.

   These include: Bricker, Calvin Jr., "Indian Atrocities Committed Against the Citizens of the Conocogheague Settlement in 1756" and "Indian Atrocities Committed Against the Citizens of the Conocogheague Settlement in 1757," unpublished, vertical file, Conococheague Institute, Mercersburg, PA, and narratives presented on a seminar and tour of the Cumberland Valley on 6-7 July 2007.

2. Quotes from Charlotte Browne are from her unpublished diary, 1754-56.

3. Quotes from Virginia, Maryland, Pennsylvania, and New York newspapers are from:

   Lucier, Armand Francis, French and Indian War Notices Abstracted from Colonial Newspapers, vol. 2: 1756-1757, Westminster, MD: Heritage Books, 2006.

4. Quotes from Washington and Sharpe are from:

   Scharf, J. Thomas, History of Western Maryland, Baltimore, MD: Clearfield Company & Family Line Publications, 1995

5. The 1756 Quebec conference quote is from:

   "Palatine, Hessian, Dutchman Three Images of the German in America" published in, Something for Everyone-Something for You, Albert F. Buffington, Don Yoder, Walter Klinefelter, Larry M. Neff, Mary Hammond Sullivan, Frederick S.Weiser, Breinigsville,PA: The Pennsylvania German Society, 1980, p-110.

6. The 1751 Maryland Committee of Grievances and Courts of Justice quote is from:

   Kessel, Elizabeth A., "The Social World of Frederick County (Maryland) Germans," A paper for the 41st Conference in Early American History of the Institute of Early American History and

Culture, Millersville, PA: April, 1981

Chapter IV "Shelter From the Storm"

1. As stated in the main text, the christening records are from the microfilm records of the Frederick German Reformed Church in the Maryland Room of the C. Burr Artz Library in Frederick, Maryland.

2. Information on Rev. Frankenfeld is from:

    Dern & Tracy, p. 151

3. All analysis in this chapter is my own.

Chapter V How The Fortified House Came to Fredericktown

1. The majority of the information on the English and Scottish origins of the fortified house came from the excellent "English Heritage PastScape website www.pastscape.org. There are links on architectural definitions of defensive buildings as well as links to the Scottish fortified house websites.

2. Descriptions of town life and defensive arrangements in the 17th-18th Century Palatinate are from:

    Eltis, David, "Towns and Defense in Later Medieval Germany," Nottingham Medieval Studies, v.33, Nottingham, Nottingham University Press, 1989

3. The document from Braddock to William Johnson is in the archives of the Pennsylvania Historical Society. Details of its content are in:

    Jennings, p. 148.

4. Research on Mohawk River Valley fortified houses was conducted on 22-23 September 2007. Special thanks are given to Alessa Wylie, Museum Coordinator at the Old Ft. Johnson Museum, Fort Johnson, NY.

5. Information on the 1970s architectural survey of Schifferstadt is from:

Milner, John D., Steenhusen, Allan H., Bourke, Jeffrey C., Schooler, Alice K., <u>Schifferstadt: A Restoration Study</u>, West Chester, Pennsylvania: National Heritage Corporation, 1974

6. Location of Carroll Creek at Schifferstadt is based on Maryland State Highway Administration plans of US 15 bypass construction.

7. German Flatts information is from the September 2007 visit and:

    Devereux, Leslie W., "Fort Hunter and the Massacre of German Flats," Utica Dispatch, takne from "Mohawk Valley History" columns published in 1932 (published date unknown.) Text compiled by Lisa Slaski, Hamilton County NYGenWeb, 2000.

Chapter VI Schifferstadt in Time of War

1. Information on historical antecedents of the interior of Schifferstadt is from:

    Ballwebber, Hattie,<u> History and Archaeology at the Schifferstadt Farmstead</u>, Columbia, MD: ACS Consultants, 1997

2. Additional information on activities at Schifferstadt is from:

    Desmond, Melanie, "Civilian Refugee Interpretation at Fort Frederick," Big Pool, MD: unpublished manuscript, Ft. Frederick State Park, 2001

3. The interpretation of the "Recreation of the Palatinate Village Culture" is based on research by Elizabeth Kessel.

    Kessel, 1981

4. Quotes from Virginia, Maryland, Pennsylvania, and New York newspapers are from:

    Lucier, 2006

5. The narrative of Armstrong's attack on Kittanning is based on a 6 July lecture at the Conococheague Institute by Jeff Wood, President of the Bosler Library, Carlisle, Pa

Chapter VII 1758

1. As stated in the main text, the primary analysis of the Treaty of Easton and Forbes campaign, as well as the quotes from Bouquet and Washington, comes from:

    Jennings, pp. 374-404, 406-410

Postscript: Pontiac's War

1. Quotes from the Maryland Gazette are from:

    Lucier, 2006

2. The quote on the use of small pox infected blankets is available from many sources. A low-keyed, but impressive presentation of this information is at the Ft. Pitt museum in Pittsburgh, Pa.

Appendix I
Location of Dunbar's Camp in Frederick

While there is limited documentation on where Dunbar's camp was located, there is one report that the primary camp was located near the current Lincoln Elementary School at the corner of South Bentz and Washington Streets. From Goldsborough (1936):

*"The route led from the **camp at the southwest part of the town** (where the Washington Street School now stands) to and across the present Harper's Ferry Road (US 340) then due west by what is now locally called "Butter Fly" Lane to the Gap at Braddock's Heights,"*

<u>The Camps Consisted of Approximately:</u>

- 700 British troops in the 48th Regiment
- Braddock's Headquarters Staff (including G. Washington)
- 200-250 Colonial Infantry
- 30 British Naval Artillery Volunteers
- 29 Pieces of Artillery with Caissons
- 50-75 Wagons with Drivers
- Sufficient Horses for the artillery, officers, & wagons.

In addition to the Goldsborough citation, the following assumptions were used to locate the boundaries of the camps.

1. The camps would have been near the lodgings and inns in Frederick, located near the intersection of All Saints and Market Streets, where meetings with Sharpe, Franklin, etc., were reported to have taken place. This intersection is just to the east of the proposed site.

2. The camps would have had to been in open areas. The area west of Fredericktown was less settled than that east toward the Monocacy River.

3. The camps would have needed access to running water. Water would have been provided by Carroll Creek, just to the north of the proposed location.

4. The camps would have been along the route of march. This is an

81

analogy that is drawn from Dunbar's July 1755 camp near Jumonville Glen, Pennsylvania.

5. The proposed size of the camps, ¾ x ¼ mile, is roughly based on Dunbar's Camp (June-July 1755) at Jumonville Glen, Pa and 18th Century drawings such as the one in the photo below.

"Confusion, Hurry and Conflagration" Dunbar's Cam

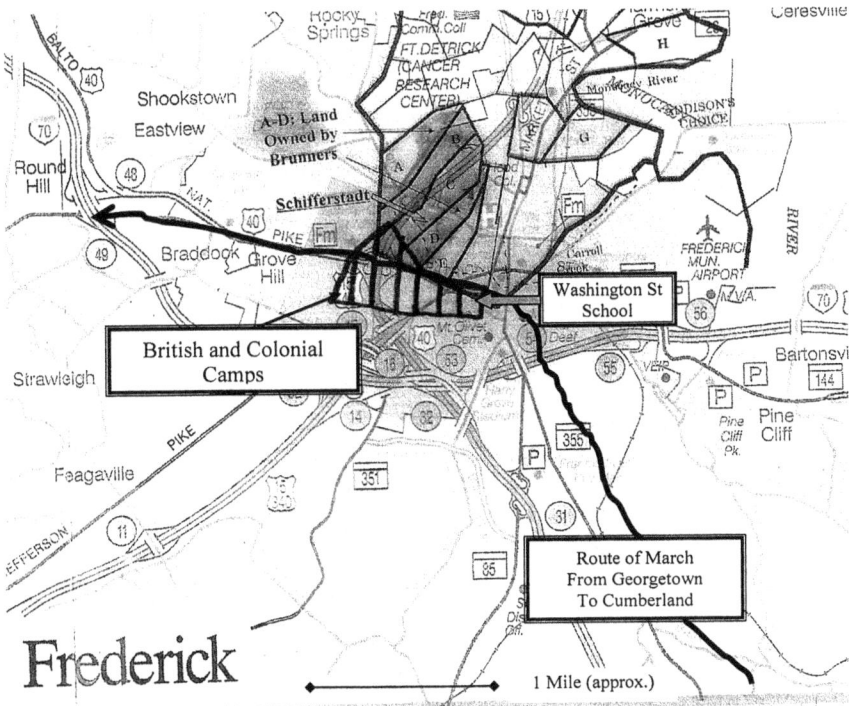

Rocky
Springs

Fred.
Comm. Coll.

FT. DETRICK
(CANCER
RESEARCH
CENTER)

Ceresville

H

Monocacy River

MADISON'S
CHOICE

Shookstown

Eastview

A-D: Land
Owned by
Brunners

Schifferstadt

G

RIVER

FREDERICK
MUN.
AIRPORT

Round
Hill

Braddock

Grove
Hill

Carroll
School

Strawleigh

**British and Colonial
Camps**

Mt. Olivet
Cem.

**Washington St
School**

Deer

Bartonsvi

Pine
Cliff
Pk.

Pine
Cliff

Feagaville

**Route of March
From Georgetown
To Cumberland**

Frederick

1 Mile (approx.)

Appendix II
Indian Attacks Within 50 Miles of Schifferstadt
(July 1755- April 1758)

Date	Location	Incident Reported/Approximate Distance
October 1755	Cresap's, Frazier's, Patterson Creek, Md	Attacks reported, no casualty lists.
Nov. 1, 1755	Great Cove (McConnellsburg) Pa	Members of 47 (out of 93) families were either killed or captured. *60 miles*
Winter 1756	Stoddert's Ft.(Hancock) Md	2 houses burned, 1 person found dead. *45 miles*
Feb 11, 1756	McDowell's Mill, Pa	3 men captured by Delaware war party. *40 miles*
Feb. 29, 1756	Little Cove, Fort David Davis, Pa, Potomac Settlements in Md	Reports of many killed and captured. *36 miles*
March 1756	Stoddert's Ft. (Hancock) Md	2 killed, from a garrison of 15. *45 miles*
Mar. 1, 1756	Ft. McDowell's Mill, Pa	Clash between militia and Indians. 5 killed and two wounded. *40 miles*
Mar. 6, 1756	Welsh Run, Pa	Studebaker family attacked. 3 killed, 3 children taken, later adopted by Indians. *35 miles*
April 1, 1756	Ft. McCord, Pa, Ft. Littleton, Pa	Ft McCord burnt. Ft. McCord militia defeated at Ft. Littleton. 21 killed, 17 wounded.
April 5, 1756	Hoops Place, Frederick Co. Md	1 captured.
May 26, 1756	Williamson, Pa	Couple attacked,1 killed, one captured, children had been left at Steel's Ft.
June, 1756	Conococheague, Pa	"Large" party of reapers killed and captured. *30-35 miles*
July, 1756	Mouth of Conococheague, Md (Williamsport, Md)	Indian attack, no casualty report. *28 miles*
July 8,	Greencastle, Allison	Rev. Steel cuts sermon short to lead

1756	Ft., Pa	congregation in pursuit of raiding party after the attack. Several killed. *30 miles*
July 20, 1756	Fort McDowell's Mill, Pa	4 killed, one captured. *40 miles*
July 26, 1756	Upton, Pa	1 killed, 2 captured. *35 miles*
July 30, 1756	Ft. Granville, Pa	Ft. Granville attacked and burned. 4 killed, 27 captured. After attack about 80% of residents in the Cumberland Valley flee eastward . *55 miles*
Aug. 27, 1756	Mouth of Conococheague, Md (Williamsport, Md)	39 killed, others captured. *28 miles*
Nov. 1, 1756	Fort McDowell's Mill, Pa	12 killed, 10 captured. *40 miles*
Dec. 1756	Ft. Loudon, Pa	Ft. Loudon is built to replace fort at McDowell's Mill. *45 miles*
Dec. 1756	Bakers, Ft Frederick, Md	"Dutch" man and women killed between Bakers and Temporary line. 1 killed at Ft. Frederick. *35-40 miles*
April 23, 1757	Fort Maxwell, Welsh Run, Pa	3 killed *35 miles*
June 9, 1757	Ft. Frederick, Md	2 waggoners killed within 1 mile of fort. *35-40 miles*
July 26, 1757	Cross' Fort (on Conoccheague Creek, about 2 miles N of Mason-Dixon line)	2 captured. John McColloh published account after his escape. *27-28 miles*
July 27, 1757	Toms Creek, Frederick, Co.	Alexander M'Keasy killed, one captured. *15 miles*
Mid-Aug. 1757	Cross' Fort	2 killed, John Kennedy wounded. *27-28 miles*
Nov. 9, 1757	Fort McDowell's Mill, Pa	3 killed, 4 children taken hostage. *40 miles*
April 13, 1758	Adams Co., Pa. (8 miles west of Gettysburg)	Baird family members killed and captured. *35 miles*

Sources

Lucier, Armand Francis, <u>French and Indian War Notices Abstracted from Colonial Newspapers, vol. 2: 1756-1757</u>, Westminster, MD: Heritage Books, 2006.

The Maryland Gazette, microfilm collection in the Maryland Room of the C. Burr Artz Library in Frederick, Maryland.

Bricker, Calvin Jr., "Indian Atrocities Committed Against the Citizens of the Conocogheague Settlement in 1756" and "Indian Atrocities Committed Against the Citizens of the Conocogheague Settlement in 1757," unpublished, vertical file, Conococheague Institute, Mercersburg, PA,

Appendix III A Short History of The Palatinate

The Palatinate is the name given to the upper Rhine valley in southwestern Germany. The modern towns of Karlsruhe and Heidelberg, Germany and Strasbourg, France are located in this region. The Thirty Years War (1618-48) is the defining historical event of the Palatinate, much as the American Civil War is for the United States.

Prior to the start of that war, the Palatinate was an important Catholic province within the Holy Roman Empire. In fact one of the Seven Electors of the Pope came from the Palatinate. In the second decade of the 17th Century, however, Calvinists (known as the Reformed Church in the United States), some moving north from Switzerland, took control of the region. This served as one of the triggers of the devastating religious and political war that was to follow.

The Thirty Years War is referred to as a religious war. Which it was: Catholic versus Protestant, mainly Lutheran and Calvinist. However, it was also a late European medieval war. In the region we now call Germany this meant a war of towns besieged and pillaged. For even by the middle 1600s, German principalities still had two defining characteristics. First, settlements were either castles or walled towns. Second, the vast majority of the population was held in serfdom by a hereditary ruling class.

The rural architecture of 17th Century England or New England that consisted of free-standing houses and barns did not, by-and-large, exist in the Palatinate because of the medieval social and economic structure. Serfs lived in the walled towns or hard by the castles and walked to the fields to toil. The walls and towers provided common protection for the elite, the emerging merchant class and the serfs. It of course fell to the serfs to build and maintain the walls and towers as well as garrison them in time of war.

The Palatinate suffered greatly during the war. Spanish forces loyal to the Church attacked from the south. Swedish forces countered from the north to restore Protestant rule. What made the war especially horrible for civilians, no matter their class, was the nature of 17th Century warfare. Nations and states were not rich enough to supply armies from their treasuries. Instead, they hired mercenaries who were paid on the basis of what they could capture and loot. Hence, towns became "targets of opportunity" based on their wealth and not necessarily on their strategic importance. What made matters worse, mercenary units were prone to quickly change sides for better looting opportunities. Suffice to say, the Palatinate was wrecked by the time the Peace of Westphalia was signed in 1648. Modern historians accept Palatinate casualties of at least thirty percent of the population killed and most towns destroyed. Except for some well-defended medieval castles that survived assaults, not much in the way of late-medieval urban Palatinate architecture remained.

Almost by design, the Peace of Westphalia did not bring peace to the Palatinate. Treaties established all towns and provinces within what is now the German, Czech, and Slovak Republics as equally sovereign. While this meant all were able to conduct diplomatic affairs, treaty provisions also prevented them from forming larger governmental units. The result was many, many poor sovereign city-states. In addition, the Palatinate was returned to Catholic Church control, meaning the remaining Protestant residents would be treated as second-class citizens at best.

These conditions of poverty and weakness left the Palatinate open as prime battlegrounds for the wars of royal succession that wracked Europe through much of the first half of the 18th Century. By the mid-1700s much of the Palatinate west of the Rhine became part of Catholic France. Serving as battlefields for these wars, while less destructive than the Thirty Years War, did not allow much in the way of reconstruction or economic opportunities for the Protestant minorities.

Palatines Come to New Amsterdam and New York

After Henry Hudson's 1609-1611 explorations in search of a Northwest Passage, the Dutch Republic granted the Dutch West India Company (a public-private stock company) rights to establish a colony in North America. Beginning in 1624, settlers arrived and established settlements from New Amsterdam (New York City) to Fort Orange (Albany), which is near the confluence of the Mohawk and Hudson Rivers.

This period of time, the 17th Century, is referred to as the Golden Age of the Netherlands. A large and active commerce fleet, protected by a modern and well-drilled navy, produced large profit margins for both private investors and the Dutch Republican government. This gave rise to the establishment of commercial banking houses and large-scale investments in both public structures and private art collections. This is the era of Rembrandt, impressive Baroque architectural achievements, and a boom in tulip bulb prices. For anyone with an interest in this very important and colorful era, Simon Schama's *The Embarrassment of Riches* is highly recommended.

Many people within the Dutch Republic also gave credit to their Calvinist religious background and its tenants of soberness, hard-work, and community for their success. For that reason, many members of the Reformed Church in Palatine found their way to Holland and later New Amsterdam as refuges from the economic and religious distress of the late 17th Century Palatinate.

In 1664, sovereignty over New Amsterdam passed to England at the end of The Second Anglo-Dutch War. However, not much would change in what was now called New York. In 1672, William of Orange became the stadholder of the Dutch Republic and quickly enlisted England as an ally against France. Furthermore, ties between Protestant groups in England and Holland began to grow. As a result of these interchanges, Dutch architects and artists came to England and visa versa. By the end of the 17th Century, English and Dutch architecture and culture was melding in many ways. Therefore, English settlers arriving in the Hudson River Valley during this time probably found the architecture fairly familiar while Dutch residents also probably had some acquaintance with English styles.

The English-Dutch union culminated in the "Glorious Revolution" of 1688 when the English Parliament offered the English Crown to the Protestant William of Orange instead of to the Catholic son of James II. (William was the husband of James II's daughter Mary who remained Protestant after her father converted to Catholicism while James II's son had been baptized a Catholic.) Confused? To continue, William III would also retain his Dutch title of stadholder along with the English Crown (which he shared with Mary) until his death in 1702.

Queen Anne (1702-1714), although an English Stuart, was also a Protestant and maintained the pro-Dutch and anti-French policies of William. Much of her reign was consumed by the War of Spanish Succession (1702-1713). And, as was becoming far too common for its residents, many of the battles in this war were also fought in the Palatinate.

Therefore, it should come as no surprise that Palatine emigration to New York expanded during her reign. While some of this was a necessary escape from war, it also appears that some personal feelings of the English monarch were involved as well. Queen Anne had become a personal patron of sorts to the Palatines. In 1709 she provided food, clothing, and housing for thousands of "Poor Palatine" (a term from that period) emigrants camped near London while they awaited transport to either Ireland or New York. It has been suggested that she saw this emigration in terms of providing Protestants with refuge from French Catholic persecution.

These new immigrants, largely indentured, first settled in the Hudson Valley but were quickly sent to work on large English owned plantations then being built on contested Indian lands in the Mohawk Valley. Besides being able to practice their religion in a Protestant based society, it was here that people from the Palatinate would first encounter a new form of warfare: Indian-European. This was a war of hit-and-run attacks by both sides, usually followed by brutal reprisals that did not distinguish between civilian and warrior populations. Terms such as scalping and hostage taking entered their vocabulary.

This type of warfare caused many of the Mohawk Valley Palatine immigrants to look to their Scottish neighbors and English landowners for ideas on how to survive in this new land. This was the background for the interactions between people such as William Johnson, Katherine Wisenberg, and the Klock family that led to the construction of fortified houses by many Palatine families.

Sources

Palmer, R.R. & Joel Colton, <u>A History of the Modern World</u>, New York: Alfred A. Knopf, 1966.

"Palatine, Hessian, Dutchman Three Images of the German in America" published in, <u>Something for Everyone-Something for You</u>, Albert F. Buffington, Don Yoder, Walter Klinefelter, Larry M. Neff, Mary Hammond Sullivan, Frederick S.Weiser, Breinigsville,PA: The Pennsylvania German Society, 1980.

Hogge, Alice, <u>God's Secret Agents</u>, New York Harper's, 2006

Appendix IV: Seven Years War Organizations and Historic Sites

The following is a list of Seven Year War historic sites and organizations commemorating the 250th anniversary of the Seven Years War. It is probably not comprehensive but it does provide a good starting point for studying those sites and artifacts still remaining from that era.

Seven Years War Organizations

The French and Indian War 250th Year Commemoration Organization
http://www.frenchandindianwar250.org/
This website provides an interactive map function to locate Seven Years War sites and maintains a calendar of Seven Years War events. A good starting point for planning any Seven Years War site visits.

The Braddock Road Preservation Association
http://www.braddockroadpa.org/
The Braddock Road Preservation Association in an advisory group on the preservation and interpretation of sites associated with Braddock's campaign and associated Seven Years War sites. They also conduct an excellent annual seminar at Jumonville, Pa every year, usually in late October or early Novemeber.

Col Washington Frontier Forts Association
http://www.fortedwards.org/cwffa/cwffhome.htm
This website provides links to Seven Years War sites associated with George Washington.

Maryland

Ft. Frederick State Park: Big Pool, MD
http://www.dnr.state.md.us/publiclands/western/fortfrederick.html

Schifferstadt: Frederick County Landmarks Foundation, Frederick, MD
www.Frederickcountylandmarksfoundation.org

New York

Fort Klock: Fort Klock Historical Society, St. Johnsville, NY
http://fortklock.org/

Fort Ticonderoga State Historic Park: Ft. Ticonderoga, NY
http://www.fort-ticonderoga.org/

Fort Stanwix National Historical Park, Ft. Stanwix, NY
http://www.nps.gov/fost/

Fort William Henry Historical Site: Lake George, NY
http://www.fwhmuseum.com/

Johnson Hall: State Historical Park, Johnstown, NY
http://nysparks.state.ny.us/sites/info.asp?siteID=17

Old Fort Johnson: Montgomery County Historical Society, Fort
Johnson, NY
http://www.oldfortjohnson.org/

Pennsylvania

Braddock's Field Historical Society
http://www.frenchandindianwar250.org/visit/details.aspx?SiteID=17
&c=

Conocogheague Institute: Welsh Run, PA
http://www.geocities.com/welshrunpa/index.html

Conrad Weiser Homestead
http://www.phmc.state.pa.us/ppet/weiserhome/page1.asp

Ft. Necessity & Jumonville National Historic Parks
http://www.nps.gov/fone/index.htm

Fort Loudon State Historic Park
http://www.fortloudoun-pa.com/

Fort Pitt Museum/Bushy Run Battle Field: Pittsburgh,PA
http://www.fortpittmuseum.com/

Pennsylvania Historic Society: Philadelphia, PA

http://www.hsp.org/default.aspx?id=620

Virginia

Carlyle House Museum: Alexandria: VA
http://www.nvrpa.org/parks/carlylehouse/index.php

Fort Edwards Historic Site: Cacapon Bridge, VA
http://www.fortedwards.org/

Ft. Loudon & George Washington's Headquarters: Winchester, VA
http://www.fortedwards.org/cwffa/gw-off.htm

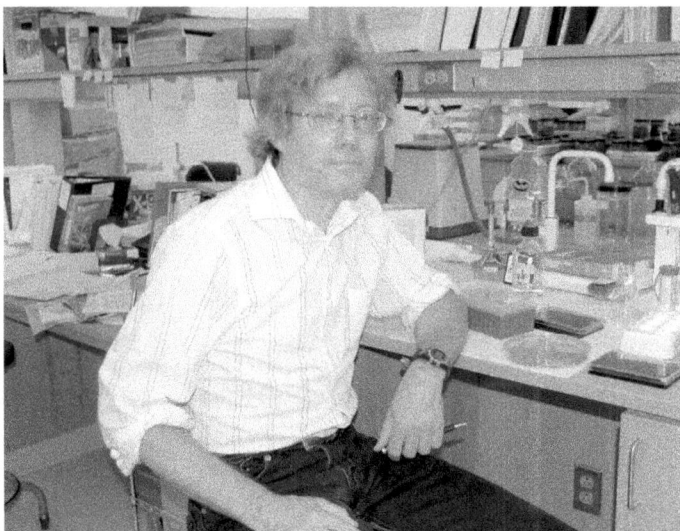

While Robert Kozak is the founder and president of a cutting-edge biotech biofuels company, Atlantic Biomass Conversions, Inc., he has a considerable background in archaeology and historic preservation as well. His specific areas of interest are World War I subchasers, the ecology of early Woodland Native Americans, and the far-reaching effects of the Seven Years War.

He was the first graduate of the George Washington University's Environmental Science Program (1975) and later led his Peace Corp fisheries development group in Western Samoa. After returning from the Peace Corps, he worked for Jimmy Carter's 1976 Presidential campaign in Ohio and Washington, D.C.

Mr. Kozak studied graduate archaeology and anthropology on scholarship at Catholic University. He has "dug" with the University of Cincinnati in the Ohio River Valley and preformed archaeology studies for the Cleveland Museum of Natural History.

As an undergraduate at George Washington University in the 1970s, he was one of the founders of "Townhouse." This Foggy Bottom historic preservation group was one of the first in the country to advocate historic preservation as a means to preserve urban neighborhoods for people of all economic classes. "Townhouse" and another D.C. pioneering group, "Don't Tear It Down," worked together to not only save buildings but to develop policies and zoning to require their creative reuse. Mr. Kozak has also renovated and restored six nineteenth and early twentieth century houses and he is a board member of the Frederick Civil War Round Table.

Mr. Kozak has worked for the Metropolitan Washington Council of Governments (COG) and D.C. Department of Transportation on vehicle emission programs. As a consultant on air quality and transportation issues, his clients included the California Air Resources Board and the States of New Jersey and Connecticut. Mr. Kozak also led an international air pollution control project in Mexico City. His Climate Change research included work on the effects of transportation water vapor (1995) for the U.S. Department of Energy/EIA.

Mr. Kozak is originally from the Cleveland, Ohio, area and spent most of his life in Washington, D.C. He now lives in Frederick, Maryland.

www.ingramcontent.com/pod-product-compliance
Lightning Source LLC
Chambersburg PA
CBHW071100090426
42737CB00013B/2411